M000102502

Very Stable Genius

The Best Words and Quotations of Donald J. Trump, Individual One, The Chosen One Volume II

Leroy Mould

ISBN:

Many Thanks and Gratitude

I am so grateful to Karin Carlson. She has been a guide, an editor, an encourager and most importantly my friend. She helped get me through this whole process.

And to my beautiful wife Maria, who has been so patient, encouraging, and inspiring: Thank you.

I also want to thank Randi Rhodes for her great work. She has encouraged me and inspired me to finish this volume.

Thank you also to Nick SanMartin for helping with the cover art and social media.

Very Stable Genius

The Best Words and Quotations of Donald J. Trump, Individual One, The Chosen One Volume II

This Time It's Serious. Believe me.

When we compiled the first volume of quotations uttered by Donald J. Trump, the intent was to show how Individual 1 thinks, speaks and demonstrates his incredible, "beautiful" grasp of issues and events. Like no one has ever done. One of the secondary effects our attempt showed was what the American people were, and, for a significant number of the populace, are willing to accept in elected leaders.

Now, in this second volume, not only have we dug up more examples of his amazing perspicacity from before November 8, 2016, but we have much more material to choose from since that momentous day.

There is a difference between Volume I and Volume II.

In Volume I, we were able to loosely fit actual quotations into general categories, like Love and Marriage, or Science, or Military. It was fairly easy to quickly turn to the one you want at a perfect moment. It's like having a portable version of Trump in your pocket any time you need a laugh.

Volume I gave us some insights. We could smile, chuckle and even laugh at the incredibly unhinged and dumb. But at the same time, it was meant to provoke us to think deeply about the kind of man or woman that we elect as President of the United States.

It is important who we elect to be President. It is important that we all vote. The result of not participating in our democracy, or not choosing well, is what we now are experiencing.

Volume II, Very Stable Genius, the Best Words of Donald J. Trump, Individual One, The Chosen One, shows a deeper view. We see and hear some of what is in his mind and his "character".

I remember during another administration that the words "character counts", were used to condemn that president for much less than what we are seeing daily.

This time it's serious. Bigly.

Love, Marriage and Family Values

(I wonder what kind of advice he gives to his children…)

To students at Liberty University:
"So I always say it, but I won't say it to you because it's a different audience, you don't want to get even, do you? Yeah, I think you do. OK. The other thing I tell people, because in New York it's like a total catastrophe, it's an epidemic. I always say, 'Always have a prenuptial agreement.' But I won't say it here because you people don't get divorced, right? Nobody gets divorced. OK, so I will not say have a prenuptial agreement to anybody in this room. I just want to end -- who else would say that, but Trump, right? I'd say -- I should say it, but I won't say it. How do I get my point across without saying it? I just did it, right? But to be a winner, and you're all winners, you've got to think like a winner, and you are just thinking like a lot of beautiful winners and I love you all. I think that's the best question."

Howard Stern show 1-11-93

1

"Dating is like being in Vietnam. Dating is like being in Vietnam. It's the equivalent of a soldier going over to Vietnam. It's like war out there. You know, if you're young and a [Inaudible] and if you have any guilt about not having gone to Vietnam, we have our own Vietnam. It's the dating [Inaudible].   Everybody becomes a star. Ivana [Inaudible] I had to keep working. No, but Ivana became a star and of course now she goes around blabbing about Donald to everybody. And she's not supposed. She got 25 million dollars to keep her stupid trap shut and to keep her mouth shut. No. Well, I'd say we're in court. I mean, it's unfortunate because I paid 25 million dollars and the one thing that she couldn't do is write books, do commercials. I mean she gets on a commercial and she says the best revenge is great colored hair, the best revenge. It's great. 25 million bucks and she's looking for revenge. I would like to have Ivana not write any more books about me. I would like to have Ivana not do any commercials, not do an interview on Barbara Walters where the first question is 'What was he really like?' Well, I don't think she badmouths me but 25 million bucks, at 25 million you're not supposed to badmouth people. Well, no, I love Ivana. She's the mother of my children."

To Barbara Walters 8-17-90
"...Yes, absolutely I do. Absolutely. I think that there's nothing better than a good marriage. There is nothing worse than a bad marriage. I'm absolutely a believer in marriage, I'm an absolute believer in fidelity. But if a marriage isn't working, that's a different ball game...." "...I am still married. I don't know what the legal definition of marriage is, to be perfectly honest...."

Prime Time live 3-10-94
"There's no such thing as divorce. You get married and that's the end of it." I agreed. I believe in marriage — one woman, one marriage. I like the image of a solid, faithfully married man. Those are the people I…"

To Howard Stern 11-9-99
"..Well, it would frighten me. But I do like the concept of marriage. I'm a great believer in marriage if you -- if you have the right woman…."

"I've always said, if you need viagra you're probably with the wrong girl."

"I don't think Ivanka would do that inside the magazine. Although she does have a very nice figure. I've said that if Ivanka weren't my daughter, perhaps I would be dating her."

In his book The Art of the Comeback
"Women have one of the great acts of all time. The smart ones act very feminine and needy, but inside they are real killers. The person who came up with the expression 'the weaker sex' was either very naive or had to be kidding. I have seen women manipulate men with just a twitch of their eye -- or perhaps another body part."

Esquire magazine interview 1991:

"You know, it doesn't really matter what they write as long as you've got a young and beautiful piece of ass."

"I like kids. I mean, I won't do anything to take care of 'em. I'll supply funds, and she'll take care of the kids." (The Howard Stern Show, April 2005)

"I've never been the kind of guy who takes his son out to Central Park to play catch, but I think I'm a good father." (Playboy, October 2004)

"But there is nothing better than having a great marriage, in my opinion. There is nothing more beautiful, and there is nothing more important." (CNN, March 21, 2004)

"I wish him luck. It's going to be a beauty." About Jeff Bezos divorce

About Melania and her birthday:
"I better not get into that because I may get in trouble. Maybe I didn't get her so much.

You know, I'm very busy- to be running out looking for presents, ok? But I got her a beautiful card and some beautiful flowers."

About Melania
"Everybody else had cloth on their face, and I probably would have also, cloth that was water, right, wet, on their face. She sat there, hey, what else is new? That's the way she is."

About the separation of children
"I think we've done an incredible job with children."

Trump: "Now, somebody who a lot of people don't give credit to but in actuality is really beautiful is Paris Hilton. I've known Paris Hilton from the time she's 12, her parents are friends of mine, and the first time I saw her she walked into the room and I said, 'Who the hell is that?'"

Stern: "Did you wanna bang her?"

Trump: "Well, at 12, I wasn't interested. I've never been into that ... but she was beautiful."

The Access Hollywood tape:

"I moved on her actually, you know she was down in Palm Beach. I moved on her and I failed. I'll admit it, I did try and fuck her. She was married. And I moved on her very heavily... I moved on her like a bitch, but I couldn't get there. All of a sudden I see her now she's got the big phony tits. She's totally changed her look.   I gotta use some tic tacs just in case I start kissing her. You know I'm automatically attracted to beautiful - I just start kissing them. It's like a magnet. When you're a star they let you do it. You can do anything. Grab em by the pussy. You can do anything."

To Brigette Trogneux, wife of French President Macron gesturing toward her body.

"You know, you're in such good shape." And then to her husband: "Beautiful"

About Katarina Witt, Olympian

"Wonderful looking while on the ice but up close and personal, she could only be described as attractive if you like a woman with a bad complexion who is built like a linebacker".

"There are basically three types of women and reactions. One is the good woman who very much loves her future husband, solely for himself, but refuses to sign the agreement on principle. I fully understand this, but the man should take a pass anyway and find someone else.
"The other is the calculating woman who refuses to sign the prenuptial agreement because she is expecting to take advantage of the poor, unsuspecting sucker she's got in her grasp. There is also the woman who will openly and quickly sign a prenuptial agreement in order to make a quick hit and take the money given to her."

To Howard Stern about having bought the Miss USA pageant:

"They said, 'How are you going to change the pageant?' I said 'I'm going to get the bathing suits to be smaller and the heels to be higher'.

"If you're looking for a rocket scientist, don't tune in tonight, but if you're looking for a really beautiful woman, you should watch."

September 12, 2019 About Melania being against vaping:

"She's got a son... together, that is a beautiful young man, and she feels very very strongly about it."

Honesty and Principles

(His idea of honesty is different from what most people think. And, principles? Hahaha- What is a principle again?)

"There is nothing that I would want more for our Country than true FREEDOM OF THE PRESS. The fact is that the Press is FREE to write and say anything it wants, but much of what it says is FAKE NEWS, pushing a political agenda or just plain trying to hurt people. HONESTY WINS!"

"I think I'm almost too honest to be a politician."
To CNN 1997

To Ted Koppel 7-21-16:
"No, the media's been very dishonest, but we put up with it. But I let people know about it. There's tremendous dishonesty in the media. But I let people know about it."

"And by the way, some are tremendously honest, but you have tremendous dishonesty in the media, tremendous. I've never seen anything like it, more so in the last number of months, I think, than I've ever seen it. With that being said, you have to power through it, and I do that. And it seems to be working out pretty well. But I do like to expose it."

"Well, I think that I'm an honest person, I feel I'm an honest person. And I don't mind being criticized at all by the media, but I do wanna -- you know, I do want them to be straight about it."

Referring to Michael Cohen:
"I know about flippers. It's called flipping, and it almost ought to be illegal. For 30,40 years I've been watching flippers. Everything's wonderful and then they get 10 years in jail and they -they flip on whoever the next highest one is, or as high as you can go. It- it almost ought to be outlawed. It's not fair."

11-21-17
"Roy Moore denies it, that's all I can say, and by the way, he totally denies it."

To Fox News 1-13-19
"I haven't actually left the White House in months."

"Somebody said I am the most popular person in Arizona because I am speaking the truth."

"Hillary Clinton may be the most corrupt person to ever seek the presidency."

During the campaign in 2016:

"But it would be interesting to see -- I will tell you this: Russia, if you're listening, I hope you're able to find the 30,000 emails that are missing. I think you will probably be rewarded mightily by our press. Let's see if that happens. That'll be next."

In March, 2019:
"Because with the fake news, if you tell a joke, if you're sarcastic, if you're having fun with the audience, if you're on live television with millions of people and 25,000 people in an arena, and if you say something like, 'Russia, please, if you can, get us Hillary Clinton's emails. Please, Russia, please. Please get us the emails. Please!'" (Crowd chants "Lock her up!") "So everybody is having a good time. I'm laughin', we're all havin' fun. And then that fake CNN and others say, 'He asked Russia to go get the emails. Horrible.' I mean, I saw it -- like, two weeks ago, I'm watching and they're talking about one of the points. 'He asked Russia for the emails.' These people are sick. And I'm telling you, they know the game. They know the game, and they play it dirty, dirtier than anybody has ever played the game. Dirtier than it's ever been played."

10-11-18
I can tell you Matt Whitaker's a great guy. I know Matt Whitaker.
11-9-18
I don't know Matt Whitaker.
11-15-18
I knew him only as he pertained, you know as he was with Jeff Sessions.

"My father is German, right? Was German, and born in a very wonderful place in Germany, so I have a great feeling for Germany," (his father was born in New Jersey)

"I think the only difference between me and the other candidates is that I'm more honest and my women are more beautiful."

"Now, the arena holds 8,000, and thank you fire department, they got in about 10. Thank you fire department, appreciate it."

Faith and Religion

(I think there's a reason why this is one of the shortest chapters)

"The Pope, I hope, can only be scared by God."

"I have a bible near my bed."

"But I pledged that, in a Trump administration, our nation's religious heritage would be cherished, protected, and defended like you have never seen before. That's what's happening. That's what's happening. You see it every day. You're reading it."

"So this morning I am honored and thrilled to return as the first sitting President* to address this incredible gathering of friends — so many friends. So many friends. And I'll ask Tony and all our people that do such a great job in putting this event together — can I take next year off or not? Or do I have to be back? I don't know."

"We are stopping cold the attacks on Judeo-Christian values.Thank you. Thank you very much. And something I've said so much during the last two years, but I'll say it again as we approach the end of the year. You know, we're getting near that beautiful Christmas season that people don't talk about anymore. They don't use the word "Christmas" because it's not politically correct. You go to department stores, and they'll say, "Happy New Year" and they'll say other things. And it will be red, they'll have it painted, but they don't say it. Well, guess what? We're saying "Merry Christmas" again."

"And we see it in the mothers and the fathers who get up at the crack of dawn; they work two jobs and sometimes three jobs. They sacrifice every day for the furniture and — future of their children. "

Brains and Knowledge

(Also a short chapter. I searched for evidence- 'Believe me')

Sept 24, 2012
"Knowledge. Knowledge. But if it's one word one words very hard for that. But the word is knowledge, but you get knowledge through experience. One of the things people talk about is luck, and I do believe that people are lucky and some people are luckier than others, I do believe that. But there's also an expression, the harder you work, the luckier you get, and I can tell you ten instances where I didn't quit, one, it was 1990, the world was coming down, the debt markets were -- everybody, all of my friends and enemies were going bankrupt, I never did.
And the -- but try -- I mean, the times were actually just terrible and even today, you look at times, and you see what happens and you have to learn. But the word luck is very interesting, but if I didn't work really hard, I probably would not, almost definitely would not be here today and unless you had me up as a man who at one point was successful, but let's see what a loser looks like."

"I'm the Ernest Hemingway of 140 characters."

"I am brainy, too brainy. I'm so intelligent it's almost unbelievable."

"I was a great student and all this stuff."

"I have a very good brain and I've said a lot of things."

"I was a great student. I was good at everything."

"I'm a thinker, and I have been a thinker. ... I'm a very deep thinker." (Palm Beach, Florida, March 11, 2016)

TRUMP: We have to prime the pump.
ECONOMIST: It's very Keynesian.
TRUMP: We're the highest-taxed nation in the world. Have you heard that expression before, for this particular type of an event?
ECONOMIST: Priming the pump?
TRUMP: Yeah, have you heard it?
ECONOMIST: Yes.
TRUMP: Have you heard that expression used before? Because I haven't heard it. I mean, I just...I came up with it a couple of days ago and I thought it was good. It's what you have to do.

"I happen to be a tariff person because I'm a smart person, OK?"

Tweeting 12/10/18

Democrats can't find a Smocking Gun tying the Trump campaign to Russia after James Comey's testimony. No Smocking Gun… No Collusion.

"No, no, I use many stats. I use many stats. You have stats that are far worse then the ones that I use, but I use many stats, but I also use Homeland Security."

"I have an attention span that's as long as it has to be."

"All of the things you're talking about, and all of the things that you're asking about, I was against at that time, and I'm still against. I haven't changed very much. Been very consistent. I'm an extremely stable genius. Ok."

Education and Such

(From the "stable genius"… and the founder of Trump University…)

"I have so many young people coming to my office where they're friends of you know, daughters and sons and all, and they want to know, can you know sit -- could you sit down with my daughter and my son and give them a little advice? I would always say study something that can help you after you get out of college. I mean, I see so many students studying things. I don't want to say anything about which because I could give you ten different names. Things that will never ever let them lead a life where they can support a family, where they can support their children and their education and healthcare and all of those things."

"I was a great student. I was good at everything."

"I love the poorly educated."

About education:

"The people running our public schools don't want to damage a student's self-esteem. They're concerned about "empowerment." They're worried kids will feel bad if they get a problem wrong or flunk a spelling test. It's better to pat a kid on the head and praise his "creative spelling" than point out that there is a traditional name for people with poor spelling skills. We call them illiterates."

"Some educators think being "judgmental" is the worst of all sins. The problem is that life tends to judge-and harshly at that. There's no room for error when you're launching the space shuttle. Or mixing the concrete for the foundation of Trump Tower, for that matter. Try giving a number "in the neighborhood of" on your tax returns and you may end up in a place where there's a very definite number stamped on the back of your shirt."

"I have a real passion for learning. My books and my professional experience always included a strong education or "lessons learned" slant. This book is a collection of my beliefs and about business and life-my basic rules and principles. It also contains questions submitted to me on the Trump University blog and my answers."

From 1987 interview with Pat Buchanan:
Buchanan: Who are your favorite authors?
Trump: Well, I have a number of favorite authors. I think Tom Wolfe is excellent.
Buchanan: Did you read Bonfire of the Vanities?
Trump: I did not.
Buchanan: It's a phenomenal book.
Tom Braden: What book are you reading now?
Buchanan: Bonfire of the Vanities.

Trump: I'm reading my own book again because I think it's so fantastic, Tom.
Buchanan: What's the best book you've read besides Art of the Deal?
Trump: I really like Tom Wolfe's last book and I think he's a great author. He's done a beautiful job.
Buchanan: Which book?
Trump: His current book, just his current book that's just out.
Buchanan: Bonfire of the Vanities?
Trump: Yes. And, uh, the man has done a very, very good job and un, I really can't hear with this earphone by the way...

About arming teachers in class rooms
"These are people, teachers in many cases, that are the highest trained that you can get. People that are natural to firearms, people that know how to handle them, people that have great experience. Also they love our students. I've seen the teachers, I see so many of them over the last two years especially , where something's happened, and they truly love their students. And by loving their students they want to fight for their students, more than anybody else would."

Meghan Kelly asked if he reads:
"Oh no, it's so long, because now I read passages. I read- I read areas, I read chapters. I just - I don't have the time."

Science and Stuff

(I am amazed at his grasp of science- very profound. I guess we should just let him solve everything.)

Speaking at a Coast Guard station in Florida- Thanksgiving 2017
"That was a big water job, right? It kept coming in and going back (About Hurricane Harvey)"
"I still haven't figured out how people take their boats out into a hurricane."
"I don't know— I mean, they go out in a boat and they think, I guess, they're - you know, they've got a wonderful boat, they've had it for years, it can weather anything."

"I was asking the Air Force guys, I said, how good is this plane? They said, well, sir, you can't see it. I said, yeah, but in a fight, you know, a fight- like I watch in the movies- they fight, they're fighting. How good is this?
Even if it's right next to it, it can't see it. I said, that helps. That's a good thing."

"Even if the Paris agreement was implemented in full, it is estimated that it would implement two-tenths of a degree of temperature reduction by 2100."

"We don't want other countries laughing at us."

"One of the problems that a lot of people like myself, we have very high levels of intelligence but we're not necessarily such believers. You look at our air and our water and it's right now at a record clean. ... As to whether or not it's man-made and whether or not the effects that you're talking about are there, I don't see it — not nearly like it is. The fire in California, where I was, if you looked at the floor, the floor of the fire they have trees that were fallen, they did no forest management, no forest maintenance, and you can light — you can take a match like this and light a tree trunk when that thing is laying there for more than 14 or 15 months, You go to other places where they have denser trees — it's more dense, where the trees are more flammable — they don't have forest fires like this, because they maintain."- speaking to the Post's Josh Dawsey and Philip Rucker.

"I'm a professional at technology."

"There's acid that can go through concrete."

"Do we want clean water? Absolutely. Do we want clean air to breathe? Absolutely. The fire in California, where I was, if you looked at the floor, the floor of the fire they have trees that were fallen, they did no forest management, no forest maintenance, and you can light -- you can take a match like this and light a tree trunk when that thing is laying there for more than 14 or 15 months. And it's a massive problem in California." And: "You need forest management, and they don't have it."

"And when you're talking about an atmosphere, oceans are very small."

"We're all committed. I'm committed, to make sure that we get all of this cleaned out and protected, take care of the floors. You know, the floors of the forests, very important. You look at other countries, where they do it differently, and it's a whole different story. I was with the president of Finland and he said, we have a much different -- we're a forest nation. He called it a forest nation, and they spent a lot of time on raking and cleaning and doing things, and they don't have any problem, and when it is, it's a very small problem."

"Oh, they're going crazy over the nice, beautiful, clean coal. And the beautiful thing is, if we have a national emergency, if we have a problem, big problem, there's nothing like coal. You'll truck that stuff around. If the roads aren't there, you'll turn it around and go through a tree. Those windmills -- number one, when the wind doesn't blow, they tend not to do too well. Right? They tend not to do too well, and they're extremely costly, and they need subsidy. We're paying massive subsidy. And of course, they kill all the birds, you know. Other than that, they're wonderful. No, they don't work too well in times of national emergency. We say, 'We need more energy, but the wind isn't blowing.' One thing with coal: that sucker, you just keep piling it in there, right? Right? Those miners. The miners knew what they were doing. And I don't want to speak badly about natural gas, because I know it. But they drop a little something on one of those pipelines --

that's the end of the natural gas, right? But the coal just keeps coming."

"I want the cleanest water on the planet. We want the cleanest air on the planet. And we've got it. But we want to keep it just that way. We've got it. Better now than ever before."

"It was all dry land. And they said -- I said, 'You must have a tremendous drought going on.' This is like, three and a half, four years ago. I said, 'You must have a tremendous drought going on.' They said, 'No, we have so much water, we don't know what to do with it. But they don't let the water come down to us.'...I know California well. And I see houses, beautiful houses -- people are very proud of their house. Their lawn is brown. It's dead. It's dying. It's dead. And they end up taking it out and just have sand in front of their houses. And they have so much water, they don't know what to do with it. It's so crazy. And you're lucky, you have the climate and you have the -- and you have the heat. But you have the water. Very few climates have that. Most climates like that don't have water; you do. You have so much you don't know what to do with it. It is a disgrace."

"Just last week, I signed a presidential memorandum to dramatically improve the reliable supply and delivery of water critical to states like California. It's one of the most ridiculous things. I saw it on the campaign trail, and I saw it numerous times. But I was out in that area -- actually with Congressman Devin Nunes, who is a terrific guy, and some of the congressmen that, right now, are out there so happy at what I signed. And I look at these incredible, beautiful fields, and they're dry. It's like dry as a bone. And I see hundreds and hundreds of acres as far as the eye could see, and then you'd have a little, tiny, little green patch in the corner. Just beautiful -- green. It's so beautiful. So rich. And I said, 'Huh, what's going on? You have this little patch, and then you have all this dry, horrible...' -- really, to me, it was horrible. It was all dry land. And they said -- I said, 'You must have a tremendous drought going on.' This is like, three and a half, four years ago. I said, 'You must have a tremendous drought going on.' They said, 'No, we have so much water, we don't know what to do with it. But they don't let the water come down to us. It naturally flows to us. They won't let it -- they send it out into the Pacific Ocean. Millions and millions and millions of gallons. We have the greatest farmland anywhere in the world, but they won't give us water. So the only areas are if we take little spots on these massive areas of land.' I could see it. I'm driving down the highway and I'm saying -- after, like, 10 minutes of looking at all this barren -- and then a little spot of beautiful. So green. I've never forgotten it. And I said, 'What's going on here?' But I assumed it was a drought. They said, 'No. The government, state and federal, send the water out into the Pacific.' I believe he said they're trying to protect a smelt. Little, tiny -- which, by the way, is doing very poorly. [Laughter] It's doing very poorly. Nobody knows what a smelt is. I still don't know what a smelt is. But it's doing very poorly. It really is a terrible thing. I said, "

"It's (Hurricane Michael) almost the entire size of the Gulf. When you look at it, topically, it's almost the entire size of the Gulf. And they haven't seen that. Maybe they haven't seen that at all. Nobody has seen that before."

"You know, we had a case just about when I was coming into office -- you all remember it -- where there was a massive -- they thought it was an earthquake. A mountain moved over an inch and a half. We're talking about mountains. You know, North Korea is very mountainous. Beautiful land. Beautiful. This mountain actually shifted. It shifted. And somebody thought it was an earthquake. And then they found out, no, this was nuclear testing. Shifted a mountain. Now I'm talking about serious stuff. Serious size."

"I'm here in the Oval Office, along with my daughter Ivanka and astronaut Kate Rubins, who recently returned from space and from the Space Station. Together, we are being joined by students all across America, thousands and thousands of students who are learning — they're learning about space, learning about a lot of other things — and they're watching this conversation from the classroom. And, all over, we have astronauts and we have everybody, who are flying right now, 17,000 miles per hour. That's about as fast as I've ever heard. I wouldn't want to be flying 17,000 miles an hour. But that's what you do."

Later in the call:

THE PRESIDENT: "Well, thank you. So well said. And I have to say, there's tremendous military application in space. We're rebuilding our military like never before. We're ordering equipment, and we're going to have the strongest military that we've ever had, the strongest military that the world has ever seen, and there's been no time where we need it more. And I'm sure that every student watching wants to know, what is next for Americans in space.

"I'm very proud that I just signed a bill committing NASA to the aim of sending America astronauts to Mars. So we'll do that. I think we'll do it a lot sooner than we're even thinking. So which one of you is ready to go to Mars? Are you ready? And I think you're ready. I know you're ready, right? We just discussed that. She'd like to go to Mars very quickly. Who's ready to go to Mars up there?"

"At my direction, the Pentagon is now working to create the sixth branch of the American armed forces, the Space Force. Very important. Very important, cutting-edge. It's all heading out to space. I hate to say it. Whether we like it or not, it's all heading out to space, so we have tremendous support. We have tremendous support. Remember all that support, Thom. We have great support. Everybody loves the space. And this is where it's at. This is where it's at. Whoa. Whoa. It's true. People get so excited with the Space Force. But that's where it's at. I'm not doing it as fun and games. That's where it's at. And I'm just talking about missiles going up or rockets going to Mars or going to -- which is very exciting. I like that. I say let the private guys do it, you know? They're all having fun. Let 'em do it. We'll rent them our great facilities. That's what we're doing. We're renting them our great facilities. Let them spend their money. They want to go to Mars, I love it. They can hop in the ship themselves. I couldn't care less. They want to do it, I'm OK with it. They're rich.I don't know, rich guys seem to like space. And I say they want to use our facilities, we'll charge them a small amount of money, like, you know, how about $25 million a launch? They'll say OK. But NASA has been reinvigorated. But we need it from the standpoint of protection, offense, defense. We need it for our military."

"And I think you saw the other day, we're reopening NASA. We're going to be going to space. Now we're going to have the Space Force because it's a whole- we need it. We need it."

"This is a tough hurricane, one of the wettest we've seen from the standpoint of water. Rarely have we had an experience like it and it certainly is not good."

"I'm an environmentalist. I want crystal-clean water. I want crystal-clean air. That's what we want."

"I mean, you know, I am a person that believes very, very strongly in the environment. I am truly an environmentalist. I know some people might not think of me as that, but I'm an environmentalist. Everything I want and every thing I have is clean. Clean is very important-water, air."

"No, no. some say that and some say differently. I mean, you have scientists on both sides of it. My uncle was a great professor at MIT for may years. Dr. John Trump. And I didn't talk to him about this particular subject, but I have a natural instinct for science, and I will say that you have scientist on both sides of the picture."

To Sean Hannity
"It's so ridiculous (the Green New Deal). No planes, let's not fly anymore. It is crazy. But personally, they should go for it. I love it."

"One of the problems that a lot of people like myself — we have very high levels of intelligence, but we're not necessarily such believers. You look at our air and our water and it's right now at a record clean. But when you look at China and you look at parts of Asia and when you look at South America, and when you look at many other places in this world, including Russia, including – just many other places — the air is incredibly dirty. And when you're talking about an atmosphere, oceans are very small. And it blows over and it sails over. I mean, we take thousands of tons of garbage off our beaches all the time that comes over from Asia. It just flows right down the Pacific, it flows, and we say where does this come from. And it takes many people to start off with.

Josh, you go to other places where they have denser trees — it's more dense, where the trees are more flammable — they don't have forest fires like this, because they maintain. And it was very interesting, I was watching the firemen and they're raking brush — you know the tumbleweed and brush and all this stuff that's growing underneath. It's on fire and they're raking it working so hard, and they're raking all this stuff. If that was raked in the beginning, there'd be nothing to catch on fire. It's very interesting to see. A lot of the trees, they took tremendous burn at the bottom, but they didn't catch on fire. The bottom is all burned but they didn't catch on fire because they sucked the water, they're wet. You need forest management, and they don't have it."

"What do you do? It's 160 miles, darling, where do I get a charge? Where do I get a charge, darling?"

"You'd be doing wind, windmills. 'Wind'. And if it doesn't -- if it doesn't blow you can forget about television for that night. Darling I want to watch television. I'm sorry, the wind isn't blowing. I know a lot about wind. I know a lot about wind."

"I support the Great Lakes, always have. They're beautiful. They're big, very deep, record deepness."

"The wheel, the wall, some things never get old."

"Even if the Paris agreement was implemented in full, it is estimated that it would implement two-tenths of a degree of temperature reduction by 2100."

To Republican leaders:
"If you have a windmill anywhere near your house, congratulations, your house just went down 75 per cent in value, And they say the noise causes cancer. You tell me that one, OK? Rerrrr rerrrr!"

About climate change:
"No. No, I have a strong opinion: I want great climate, we're going to have that."

"For all of the money we are spending, NASA should NOT be talking about going to the Moon - We did that 50 years ago. They should be focused on the much bigger things we are doing, including Mars (of which the Moon is a part), Defense and Science!"

"... and of course it's like a grave yard for birds. If you love birds, you'd never want to walk under a windmill because it's a very sad, sad sight. It's like a cemetery. We put a little statue for the poor birds. It's true. You know in California if you shoot a bald eagle they put you in jail for five years. And yet the windmills they wipe them all out. It's true. They wipe them out. It's terrible."

"No, wind's not so good and you have no idea how expensive it is to make those things. They're all made in China and Germany, by the way, just in case you, we don't make them here, essentially."

Trump, Aug. 30: Clean power, right? They want to have windmills all over the place, right? When the wind doesn't blow, what do we do? Uh, we got problems. When there's thousands of birds laying at the base of the windmill, what do we do? Isn't that amazing? The environmentalists, "We like windmills." Oh, really? What about the thousands of birds they're killing? Try going to the bottom of a windmill someday. It's not a pretty picture. But, really, when the wind doesn't blow, you got problems. If your house is staring at a windmill, not good. When you hear that noise going round and round and round, and you're living with it, and then you go crazy after a couple of years, not good. And the environmentalists say, oh, isn't it wonderful? 8/30/18

September 12, 2019:
"The light bulb. People said what's with the light bulb. I said here's the story, and I looked at it. The bulb that we're being forced to use. Number one, to me, most importantly, the light's no good. I always look orange. And so do you. The light is the worst."

History

(Those who do not learn from history are doomed to repeat it, or at least make it all up!)

"The reason Russia was in Afghanistan was because terrorists were going into Russia. They were right to be there. The problem is it was a tough fight."

"We are talking to the Taliban. We're talking to a lot of different people. But here's the thing -- because you mentioned India: India is there. Russia is there. Russia used to be the Soviet Union. Afghanistan made it Russia, because they went bankrupt fighting in Afghanistan…They were right to be there. The problem is it was a tough fight. And literally, they went bankrupt. They went into being called Russia again, as opposed to the Soviet Union. You know, a lot these places you're reading about now are no longer a part of Russia because of Afghanistan."

"People don't realize. You know, if you go back to the Civil War, it was the Republicans that really did the thing."

Tweet 5-1-16
President Andrew Jackson, who died 16 years before the Civil War started, saw it coming and was angry. Would never have let it happen!

"The 1990's sure aren't like the 1980's."

Feb 7 2019 at National Prayer breakfast:
"Since the founding of our nation, many of our greatest strides, from gaining our independence to abolition of civil rights to extending the vote for women, have been led by people of faith"

Q: Mr. President
DJT: You okay?
Q: I am. Just wanted to get untangled. Very simply, you said today that you had the biggest electoral margins since Ronald Reagan with 304 or 306 electoral votes. In fact, President Obama got 365 in 2008.
DJT: Well, I'm talking about Republican. Yes.
Q: President Obama, 332. George H.W. Bush, 426 when he won as President. So why should Americans trust-
DJT: Well, no, I was told- I was given that information. I don't know. Was just given. We had a very, very big margin.
Q: I guess my question is, why should Americans trust you when you have accused the information they receive of being fake when you're providing information that's fake?
DJT: Well, I don't know. I was given that information. I was given- actually, i've seen that information around. But it was a very substantial victory. Do you agree with that?
Q: You're the President.
DJT: Okay, thank you. That's a good answer. Yes.

With Meet The Press
"It is better to live one day as a lion than 100 years as a sheep," Trump tweeted a quote of Mussolini.
"It's a very good quote, It's a very interesting quote, and I know it. I saw it... What difference does it make whether it's Mussolini or somebody else? It's certainly a very interesting quote."

Chuck Todd:"Do you want to be associated with a fascist?"

"No,I want to be associated with interesting quotes."

A Times reporter asked about the plaque on his golf course that falsely claims a Civil War battle took place there:

"Write your story the way you want to write it. ... You don't have to talk to anybody. It doesn't make any difference. But many people were shot. It makes sense."

About Abraham Lincoln:
"Most people don't even know he was a Republican," Trump said. "Does anyone know? Lot of people don't know that!"

"You know when Abraham Lincoln made the Gettysburg Address speech- the great speech- you know he was ridiculed. He was ridiculed. He took the horse and carriage up from the White House. He wrote it partially in that carriage and partially at a desk in the Lincoln Bedroom, which is incredible by the way in the White House. And he went up to Gettysburg and he delivered that speech- the Gettysburg Address- and he was excoriated- by the fake news- they had fake news then- he was excoriated. They said it was a terrible, terrible speech. They said it was far too short. It's not long. Many of us know it by memory. It was far too short and it was far too flowery. It was too flowery. "Four score and seven years ago"- right? And he died.

"Fifty years after his death they said it may have been the greatest speech ever made in America. Pretty good. Pretty good. I have a feeling that's going to happen with us. In different ways that's gonna happen with us. For years you watched as your leaders apologized to other countries for America. We apologize. We're so sorry. So sorry. So sorry. Now you have a president* who's standing up for our country. I'm standing up."

On July 4th, 2019:
"In June of 1775, the Continental Congress created a unified army out of the revolutionary forces encamped around Boston and New York, and named after the great George Washington, Commander-in-Chief. The Continental Army suffered a bitter winter of Valley Forge, found glory across the waters of the Delaware, and seized victory from Cornwallis of Yorktown. Our army manned the air, it rammed the ramparts, it took over the airports, it did everything it had to do. And at Fort McHenry, under the rockets' red glare, it had nothing but victory. And when dawn came, their star-spangled banner waved defiant."

10-9-19
The Kurds are fighting for their land, just so you understand, and somebody wrote a very, very powerful article today. They didn't help us in the Second World War, they didn't hep us with Normandy as an example, they mentioned names of different battles. But they're here to help us with their land and that's a different thing. In addition to that we- we have spent tremendous amounts of money on helping the Kurds in terms of ammunition, in terms of weapons, in terms of

money, in terms of pay, with all that being said, we like the
Kurds.

The Military and War

(It's like a game! And with really cool stuff!)

With Rona Barrett- 1980
About the Iran Iraq war:
DT:No, I don't see a war. You see the war is -- this is not a
Vietnam situation fortunately. The war in fact with Iraq —
RB:There is a war raging there right now.
DT:Oh yes, there is a war, and it's a war where nobody has
any tanks, has any guns. It's a war where everyone is standing
around. That would have been the easiest victory we would
have ever won, in my opinion.
RB: Well, when I look at television, I see men being shot up
like being blown off.
DT: But you're talking about two non-existent armies. I mean
Iran has an army composed of American equipment without
parts and without anything else, and Iraq has a very weak
army, and they're just really fighting each other, and it's
almost hand-to-hand combat if you see now. It's a sad
situation, Rona, but it's a situation which ultimately is going
to get much worse. That little sparkle of war, that little
sparkle, is going to lead in my opinion to a much, much

greater conflict, and I think that's very unfortunate. I think a lot of it has to do with this country and the fact that this country is not more involved in terms of setting policy in that area.

Speaking at a Coast Guard station in Florida- Thanksgiving 2017
"I was asking the Air Force guys, I said, how good is this plane? They said, well, sir, you can't see it. I said, yeah, but in a fight, you know, a fight- like I watch in the movies- they fight, they're fighting. How good is this?
"Even if it's right next to it, it can't see it. I said, that helps. That's a good thing."

"And you just saw that because you just got one of the biggest pay raises you've ever received -- unless you don't want it. Does anybody here -- is anybody here willing to give up the big pay raise you just got? Raise your hands, please. Ah, I don't see too many hands. Okay, don't give it up. It's great. You know what? Nobody deserves it more. You haven't gotten one in more than 10 years -- more than 10 years. And we got you a big one. I got you a big one. I got you a big one. They had plenty of people that came up. They said, 'You know, we could make it smaller. We could make it 3 per cent. We could make it 2 per cent. We could make it 4 per cent.' I said, 'No. Make it 10 per cent. Make it more than 10 per cent.' Because it's been a long time. It's been more than 10 years. It's been more than 10 years. That's a long time."

THE PRESIDENT: Well, thank you. So well said. And I have to say, there's tremendous military application in space. We're rebuilding our military like never before. We're ordering equipment, and we're going to have the strongest military that we've ever had, the strongest military that the world has ever seen, and there's been no time where we need it more. And I'm sure that every student watching wants to know, what is next for Americans in space.

"At my direction, the Pentagon is now working to create the sixth branch of the American armed forces, the Space Force. Very important. Very important, cutting-edge. It's all heading out to space. I hate to say it. Whether we like it or not, it's all heading out to space, so we have tremendous support. We have tremendous support. Remember all that support, Thom. We have great support. Everybody loves the space. And this is where it's at. This is where it's at. Whoa. Whoa. It's true. People get so excited with the Space Force. But that's where it's at. I'm not doing it as fun and games. That's where it's at. And I'm just talking about missiles going up or rockets going to Mars or going to -- which is very exciting. I like that. I say let the private guys do it, you know? They're all having fun. Let 'em do it. We'll rent them our great facilities. That's what we're doing. We're renting them our great facilities. Let them spend their money. They want to go to Mars, I love it. They can hop in the ship themselves. I couldn't care less. They want to do it, I'm OK with it. They're rich.I don't know, rich guys seem to like space. And I say they want to use our facilities, we'll charge them a small amount of money, like, you know, how about $25 million a launch? They'll say OK. But NASA has been reinvigorated. But we need it from the standpoint of protection, offense, defense. We need it for our military."

Nov. 24, 2017, Thanksgiving, to the Coast Guard

"But if you were looking at it as a brand, there's no brand that went up more than the Coast Guard with what happened in Texas.

You saved 16,000 lives— nobody knows that— 16,000 lives. Your whole, long life, the stock market is higher than it's ever been. And that means your 401(k), all of the things that you have, whether it's even if you're in the military, you have a country that's really starting to turn.

You know, when we sell to other countries, even they're allies- you never know about an ally. An ally can turn. A little bit- keep a little bit - keep about 10% in the bag, because what we have- nobody has like what we have, and that's what we're doing."

"And I think you saw the other day, we're reopening NASA. We're going to be going to space. Now we're going to have the Space Force because it's a whole- we need it. We need it."

At a campaign event at a retirement village in South Carolina:

"Don't tell me it doesn't work — torture works. Half these guys [say]: 'Torture doesn't work.' Believe me, it works. They're chopping off our heads in the Middle East. They want to kill us, they want to kill us. They want to kill our country. They want to knock out our cities.

Some people say it's not actually torture — let's assume it is. But they asked me the question: 'What are you going to do on waterboarding?' Absolutely fine, but we should go much stronger than waterboarding. That's the way I feel."

"We have some of our great business leaders — and leaders period — right behind me,"

Trump said at the lectern before asking Hewson to say a few words: "I may ask Marillyn Lockheed, the leading women's business executive in this country, according to many, We buy billions and billions of dollars worth of that beautiful F-35. It's stealth. You cannot see it. Is that correct? It better be correct,"

AP: Can I ask you, over your first 100 days — you're not quite there yet — how do you feel like the office has changed you?

TRUMP: Well the one thing I would say — and I say this to people — I never realized how big it was. Everything's so (unintelligible) like, you know the orders are so massive. I was talking to —

AP: You mean the responsibility of it, or do you mean —

TRUMP: Number One, there's great responsibility. When it came time to, as an example, send out the 59 missiles, the Tomahawks in Syria. I'm saying to myself, "You know, this is more than just like, 79 (sic) missiles. This is death that's involved," because people could have been killed. This is risk that's involved, because if the missile goes off and goes in a city or goes in a civilian area — you know, the boats were hundreds of miles away — and if this missile goes off and lands in the middle of a town or a hamlet .... every decision is much harder than you'd normally make. (unintelligible) ... This is involving death and life and so many things. ... So it's far more responsibility. (unintelligible) ....The financial cost of everything is so massive, every agency. This is thousands of times bigger, the United States, than the biggest company in the world. The second-largest company in the world is the Defense Department. The third-largest company in the world is Social Security. The fourth-largest — you know, you go down the list.

AP: Right.

TRUMP. It's massive. And every agency is, like, bigger than any company. So you know, I really just see the bigness of it all, but also the responsibility. And the human responsibility. You know, the human life that's involved in some of the decisions.

They had a quote from me that NATO's obsolete. But they didn't say why it was obsolete. I was on Wolf Blitzer, very fair interview, the first time I was ever asked about NATO, because I wasn't in government. People don't go around asking about NATO if I'm building a building in Manhattan, right? So they asked me, Wolf ... asked me about NATO, and I said two things. NATO's obsolete — not knowing much about NATO, now I know a lot about NATO — NATO is obsolete, and I said, "And the reason it's obsolete is because of the fact they don't focus on terrorism." You know, back when they did NATO there was no such thing as terrorism.

"When I got in here, you were having jet fighters that were so old -- you know, you heard the story -- the grandfather flew some of the planes -- some of the bombers. The grandfather, then the son, then the grandchild is here with us now. And I don't like that. I don't like that. So we've ordered massive numbers of new planes and new everything."

"Nobody's done more for the military than I have. I took the budget from very little to $700 billion- $716 billion and I'm now going over to the Coast Guard where I did last year and will probably a lot. But we're going over to the Coast Guard and I just really believe nobody in fact a number of generals were on television over the weekend, unrelated, but they all mentioned that nobody's done as a president for the military in a long time what I've done."

Question about troops at the border.
"No -no troops. We're going to have a strong border. Our southern border is going to be very strong… you gotta have borders. You don't have borders you don't have a country."

What about the military using lethal force?
"They're going to have to use lethal force- I've given the okay."

"When I came into office people thought we were going into nuclear war, OK and now they're saying wow."

About a strategy to defeat ISIS:
AP: Can you say generally what the strategy is? Should people
—

TRUMP: Generally is we have got to get rid of ISIS. We have no choice. And other terrorist organizations.

AP: Should Americans who are serving in the military expect that you are going to increase troop numbers in the Middle East to fight ISIS?

TRUMP: No, not much.

AP: In terms of the strategy, though, that you have accepted, it sounds like, from the generals —

TRUMP: Well, they've also accepted my strategy.

AP: Does that involve more troops on the ground, it sounds like?

TRUMP: Not many.

AP: So a small increase?

TRUMP: It could be an increase, then an increase. But not many more. I want to do the job, but not many more. ... This is an important story. I've done a lot. I've done more than any other president in the first 100 days and I think the first 100 days is an artificial barrier. And I'm scheduled ... the foundations have been set to do some great things. With foreign countries. Look at, look at President Xi. I mean …

About Syria January 2, 2019:
"We're talking about sand and death. That's what we're talking about."

"I had a meeting at the Pentagon with lots of generals. They were like from a movie. Better looking than Tom Cruise, and stronger. And I had more generals than I've ever seen, and we were at the bottom of this incredible room. I said "this is the greatest room I've even seen.""

Foreign Relations

(If you can figure these out, you can figure out his foreign policy.)

"He treated me better than anybody's ever been treated in the history of China."
(In the history of China.)
"One of the great two days of anybody's life and memory having to do with China."

8/26/15 campaign event in Iowa—- while imitating Asian speakers:

"When these people walk into the room, They don't say, 'Oh hello, how's the weather? It's so beautiful outside. How are the Yankees doing? They're doing wonderful, that's great.' They say, 'We want deal!'"

"The world went crazy when the Paris agreement was signed. They went wild. This was because it placed America at a serious economic disadvantage."

"I was elected to represent the citizens of Pittsburgh, not Paris."

"We don't want other countries laughing at us."

"So Mexico is paying for the wall indirectly."

"Iran is not the same country since I took away the -- you know, the -- you know, it's a different country...Their economy has crashed. Their currency has crashed. They're having riots every week, big ones, in every city."

"As we speak, Democrats are openly encouraging millions of illegal aliens to break our laws..."
"That's what they want. Democrats are inviting caravan after caravan of illegal aliens to pour into our country, overwhelming your schools, your hospitals, and your communities."

"Obama paid (Iran) $1.8 billion and he gave $150 billion."

"So we like South Korea. We've got 32,000 soldiers over there. Thank you very much, United States. They don't pay. They don't pay us, but that's OK. They're very successful."

3-15-18— Friends of Ireland luncheon
"Thank you very much, Paul, and Vice President Pence, distinguished members of Congress, so many wonderful people from Ireland. So many friends, and we appreciate it — for joining us on this very special occasion. It really is. First time was last year, and I still remember — I said, "That was a

lot of fun." We'll do it — I guess, what do we have? Six more left after this."

On who's been the toughest on Russia:
"You can ask President Putin about that. There's been nobody. So there's no collusion whatsoever."

About North Korea and Kim Jong Un:
"Look, it was very, very nasty with Little Rocket Man and with the buttons-and, you know, my button's bigger than-everybody said this guy's going to get us into nuclear war. The nuclear war would have happened if you had weak people.
He will turn that country into a great successful country. And the fact that we do get along means we are safe, and I'm not saying that things can happen, things go wrong and mistakes are made, relationships get broken. But right now, you are so safe."

"I'll tell you something, we want to get along with Russia. But Russia is looking out and they're saying, "Man, I wish she won.""

"Because we spent $7 trillion in the Middle East. Now if you wanna fix window some place they say, "oh gee, let's not do it". Seven trillion and millions of lives- you know, 'cause I like to count both sides. Millions of lives.
To me, it's the worst single mistake made in the history of our country. Civil war you can understand. Civil war, civil war. That's different. For us to have gone into the Middle East, and that was just, that was a bad day for this country, I will tell you."

About the Kashoggi murder
"He did not know about it and it sounded like, you know the concept of rogue killers.
You know, here we go again with, you know, you're guilty until proven innocent. I don't like that."

"Every country takes advantage of us, almost. I may be able to find a couple that don't. But for the most part, that would be a very tough job for me to do.
But things change. There has to be flexibility. Let me give you an example. President Xi, we have a, like, a really great relationship. For me to call him a currency manipulator and then say, "By the way, I'd like you to solve the North Korean problem," doesn't work. So you have to have a certain flexibility, Number One. Number Two, from the time I took office till now, you know, it's a very exact thing. It's not like generalities. Do you want a Coke or anything?"
"And the media, some of them get it, in all fairness. But you know some of them either don't get it, in which case they're very stupid people, or they just don't want to say it. You know because of a couple of them said, "He didn't call them a currency manipulator." Well, for two reasons. Number One, he's not, since my time. You know, very specific formula. You would think it's like generalities, it's not. They have — they've actually — their currency's gone up. So it's a very, very specific formula. And I said, "How badly have they been," ... they said, "Since you got to office they have not manipulated their currency." That's Number One, but much more important, they are working with us on North Korea. Now maybe that'll work out or maybe it won't. Can you imagine? ..."

TRUMP: Look, he turned down many coal ships. These massive coal ships are coming where they get a lot of their income. They're coming into China and they're being turned away. That's never happened before. The fuel, the oil, so many different things. You saw the editorial they had in their paper saying they cannot be allowed to have nuclear, you know, et cetera. People have said they've never seen this ever before in China. We have the same relationship with others. There's a great foundation that's built. Great foundation. And I think it's going to produce tremendous results for our country.

"China can do whatever they want. They can build coal plants, and we can't."

"Human trafficking is a disaster. Nobody knew much about it until recently. It's been going on for a million years actually. It's been going on for a long time. But we've seen it- we've spotted it."

From a cabinet meeting / press answering questions
"And- we've made tremendous progress with North Korea. When I came in- or lets say at the end of the last administration, frankly it looked like we were going to war with North Korea. Now, there's no missile testing, there's no rocket testing, there's no nuclear testing. We got back our prisoners or our hostages, and we're getting back our remains- they're coming in. And we've had some beautiful ceremonies in Hawaii and other places. So I just tell you that we are doing really well- our military is being rebuilt- it's very close to being rebuilt- tremendous amounts of new aircraft-new ships-new weapons of all kinds which we need because hopefully the stronger you get the less you have to

use it. I guess you know that from growing up in school.....
so I didn't see the report from the intelligence -it's a lot
different when you read it from when it's covered by the news
and on television."

About Putin:
"He doesn't respect our president. And if it is Russia -- which
it's probably not, nobody knows who it is - but it if is Russia,
it's really bad for a different reason. Because it shows how
little respect they have for our country when they would hack
into a major party and get everything. But it would be
interesting to see -- I will tell you this: Russia, if you're
listening, I hope you're able to find the 30,000 emails that are
missing. I think you will probably be rewarded mightily by
our press. Let's see if that happens. That'll be next."

"And I told Guatemala and I told Honduras, and I told El
Salvador -- three places where they send us tremendous
numbers of people -- and they're rough people. They're not
sending us their finest. It doesn't make sense. Why would
they send their finest? They're sending us some very -- as I
would sometimes say -- rough hombres. These are rough,
rough, tough people. Many criminal people."

"When President Obama pulled out of Iraq in theory we had
Iraq. In other words, we had Iraq. We never had Syria because
President Obama never wanted to violate the red line in the
sand. So we never had Syria. I was the one that actually
violated the red line when I hit Syria with 59 Tomahawk
missiles, if you remember. But President Obama chose not to
do that. When he chose not to do that, he showed tremendous
weakness. But we didn't have Syria whereas we had Iraq."

What about the military using lethal force?

"They're going to have to use lethal force- I've given the okay.

Bad things are happening in Tijuana. But not in this country, because I closed it up I actually two days ago we closed the border. We actually just closed it. We said nobody's coming in because it was so out of control.

And Mexico will not be able to sell their cars into the United States where they make so many cars at great benefit to them, not at great benefit to us.

I've already shut it down (the border) - I've already shut it down- for short periods. I've already shut down parts of the border because it was out of control with the rioting on the other side in Mexico. I just said shut it down. You see it. It took place two days ago. Yeah- they call me up and I sign an order."

"Can we get a copy of that?"

"Aaah— you don't need that. Don't worry- it's not that big a deal. But maybe to some people it is."

Wall Street Journal interview 11/27/18:

"I happen to be a tariff person because I'm a smart person, OK? We have been ripped off so badly by people coming in and stealing our wealth. The steel industry has been rebuilt in a period of a year because of what I've done. We have a vibrant steel industry again, and soon it'll be very vibrant. You know, they're building plants all over the country because I put steel — because I put tariffs, 25 percent tariffs, on dumping steel."

About Saudi Arabia- same interview

"But they've been a great ally. Without them, Israel would be in a lot more trouble. We need to have a counterbalance to Iran. I know him. I know him well, the Crown Prince. And, by the way, never did business with them, never intend to do business with them. I couldn't care less. This is a very important job that I'm doing right now. The last thing I care about is doing business with people. I only do business for us. Somebody said, well, maybe they're an investor in one of his jobs. The answer is no. But I just feel that it's very, very important to maintain that relationship."

He also revealed he had called authoritarian Chinese president Xi Jinping a "king" during a visit to Beijing in 2017.
"He said, 'But I am not king, I am president'. I said, 'No, you're president for life, and therefore you're king'," Then laughter. "He said, huh. He liked that. I get along with him great."

"China. China. We've gone up. They've gone down but we want them to be healthy.
China and by the way we are building that wall as you -- we are building that wall. Build it.
It's faster and it's less expensive and it's also much more beautiful.
They do anything they can -- you're a shifty shift."

10-16-19
With the president of Italy
"A lot of sand- they've got a lot of sand over there.
Where is the server? How come the FBI never got the server?
Where is the server? I wanna see the server. Let's see what's on the server. I'd like to see the server- to see the server. I

don't know- that's up to him. That you have to ask- excuse me, no. They never dealt, John, with the Democrats the way the Democrats deal. And the Republicans won't forget it. People like him are.. I don't even know who they are. I've never even heard of some of 'em. You go to Europe and the roads are opposite."

10-7-19

Tweet

As I have stated strongly before, and just to reiterate, if Turkey does anything that I, in my great and unmatched wisdom, consider to be off limits, I will totally destroy and obliterate the Economy of Turkey (I've done before!)

10-9-19

"The Kurds are fighting for their land, just so you understand, and somebody wrote a very, very powerful article today. They didn't help us in the Second World War, they didn't hep us with Normandy as an example, they mentioned names of different battles. But they're here to help us with their land and that's a different thing. In addition to that we- we have spent tremendous amounts of money on helping the Kurds in terms of ammunition, in terms of weapons, in terms of money, in terms of pay, with all that being said, we like the Kurds."

Minutes before a meeting with President Zelensky
"It's a great thing. And we had a winner from Ukraine." (No Ukranian woman has ever won Miss Universe.)

"Germany does almost nothing for you. All they do is talk."
To Zelensky on the July 25 call.

"I want to see other countries helping Ukraine also, not just us. As usual the United States helps and nobody else is there. I'd withhold again, and I'll continue to withhold until such time as Europe and other nations contribute to Ukraine. Because they're not doing it; it's the United States. ... Why is it only the United States putting up the money?"

Politics

(So——- this should be interesting, and revealing. Just remember and consider he really said all of these. A window into the way this president* thinks. Political opponents should study this stuff.)

"I think I'm almost too honest to be a politician."
To CNN 1997

"I can only tell you that there is absolutely no collusion. Everybody knows it. And you know who knows it better than anybody? The Democrats. They walk around blinking at each other." To Michael Schmidt 12-28-17

"I'm the one that saved coal."

"Hey, let's get together. Let's do bipartisan."

"We hear bullshit from the Democrats. Like Joe Manchin. Joe's a nice guy."

"I have unbelievably great relationships with 97% of the Republican congressmen and senators. I love them and they love me."

"No, I'm not being centered. I'm always moving. I'm moving in both directions."

"I will build a great wall -- and nobody builds walls better than me, believe me --and I'll build them very inexpensively. I will build a great, great wall on our southern border, and I will make Mexico pay for that wall. Mark my words."

Announcing his candidacy June 2015:
"Our country is in serious trouble. We don't have victories anymore. We used to have victories, but we don't have them. When was the last time anybody saw us beating, let's say China, in a trade deal? I beat China all the time. All the time."

March 2011 on the phone w Fox & Friends:
"I dealt with Qaddafi. I rented him a piece of land. He paid me more for one night than the land was worth for two years, and then I didn't let him use the land. That's what we should be doing. I don't want to use the word 'screwed', but I screwed him. That's what we should be doing."

4-25-16
"You know, I tweeted today— @realDonaldTrump, I tweet. You know that solves it. Don't worry I'll give it up after I'm president. We won't tweet anymore…not presidential

It's going to be made of hardened concrete and it's going to be made out of rebar. That's steel. And we're going to set the rebar in nice heavy foundations."

In an interview with The Economist:
TRUMP: We have to prime the pump.
ECONOMIST: It's very Keynesian.
TRUMP: We're the highest-taxed nation in the world. Have you heard that expression before, for this particular type of an event?
ECONOMIST: Priming the pump?
TRUMP: Yeah, have you heard it?
ECONOMIST: Yes.
TRUMP: Have you heard that expression used before? Because I haven't heard it. I mean, I just...I came up with it a couple of days ago and I thought it was good. It's what you have to do.

"The fact is, if we don't have barriers, walls, call it what you want, we don't have very strong barriers, where people can not, any longer, drive right across. They have unbelievable vehicles. They make a lot of money, they have the best vehicles you can buy. They have stronger, bigger and faster vehicles than our police have, and that ICE has, and that the Border Patrol has."

"So we're going to Texas. We're going to the border. Just spoke to some of my friends in Arizona. We have tremendous support."

"The Republicans are extremely united. They all want to see something happen, but they're extremely united."

"For instance, this morning a number of people came out and said, 'You do need very strong border security, and that includes a wall or whatever it is.' A number of Democrats said that, but people don't like to report on it."

"We have tremendous unity in the Republican Party. It's really a beautiful thing to see. I don't think there'll be any breakaway, because they know we need border security and we have to have it.
When during the campaign I would say, 'Mexico's going to pay for it,' obviously I never said this and I never meant they're going to write out a check."

"They've been taken over by a group of young people who, frankly, in some cases -- I've been watching -- I actually think they're crazy.

"And I find China, frankly, in many ways, to be far more honorable than Cryin' Chuck and Nancy. I really do."

"I think that China is actually much easier to deal with than the opposition party."

"I have the absolute right to declare a national emergency."

"I haven't done it yet. I may do it. If this doesn't work out, probably I will do it ... I would almost say definitely."

"And they don't come in at the checkpoints, which they do also."

"If we don't make a deal -- I mean, I would say a hundred percent, but I don't want to say a hundred percent, because maybe something else comes up."

"If we don't make a deal, I would say it would be very surprising to me that I would not declare a national emergency and just fund it through the various mechanisms."

"I don't know if they know how to make a deal."

"But that's a wall, and they have other walls. We have many walls under consideration."

"I very calmly said, 'If you're not going to give us strong borders, bye-bye.' And I left. I didn't rant. I didn't rave, like you reported."

"We have to come up, and we can come up with many different plans. In fact, plans you don't even know about will be devised because we're going to come up with plans- healthcare plans - that will be so good."

"Free trade can be wonderful if you have smart people, but we have people that are stupid."

"Here's one that I love -- here's one that I love: the Hispanic -- Hispanic American, African-American -- Kanye West, was he great? He did me a big favor. Kanye! People like him -- and Asian-American unemployment have all reached their lowest rates ever recorded... Think of that. Unemployment. African-American, Hispanic American, Asian-American -- lowest ever."

"There's a town in California where they actually tried to take over the town council. All illegal aliens running the town council. That sounds like a great idea."

"And a sad thing happened last week. Because Elizabeth Warren was exposed as being a total fraud. And I can no longer call her Pocahontas, because she has no Indian blood! I can't call her... I can't call her Pocahontas. She doesn't qualify. She has -- I've been saying for a long time. I've been saying it for a year-and-a-half, I said I have more Indian blood than she has, and I have none. I have none. But I have more than she has. But I can't use the name Pocahontas anymore. But if you don't mind, I will anyway. Is that OK? We got to keep her down."

"He (Beto O'Rourke) got an F from the NRA, one of the few. You know -- you know what an F means? An F means he wants to take away your guns, OK? That's what it means. I never even heard of an F. I never heard. Louie, did you ever hear of an F?"

"How about in California, where illegal immigrants took over the town council, and now the town council is run by illegal immigrants in the town! I mean, is this even believable? You tell this stuff. It is sick!"

"It is amazing how you can delete 33,000 e-mails after getting a subpoena from the United States Congress and our Justice Department doesn't do anything about it. It is pretty amazing. Our Justice Department. Headed by many people from the Obama administration.
You know another thing we did for -- I like a lot of people in Arizona, small businesses, farmers. You don't have estate tax.

No more estate tax. So if you love your children -- which is a question -- you may not like 'em, in which case don't listen to me -- if you don't like 'em, don't leave them the farm. But if you love 'em, you'll love Trump, because you don't have to pay estate tax, OK? That's a big thing."

"Fake news. But a lot of money has been passing to people to come up and try and get to the border by Election Day, because they think that's a negative for us."

"It's nothing more than a witch hunt. And most people get it, including Democrats. They wink at me. They look at me, they wink at me. The Democrats get it too.
In fact, I've been going around lately saying the Democrats are the party of crime. And nobody even challenges me, not even the fake news media. They don't even challenge me."

"The Democrats want to erase America's borders and let drugs, gangs and crime pour into our country.
And I've seen it, I've had friends talk about it when people get in line that have absolutely no right to vote and they go around in circles. Sometimes they go to their car, put on a different hat, put on a different shirt, come in and vote again. Nobody takes anything. It's really a disgrace what's going on."

"I'll give you voter suppression: Take a look at the CNN polls, how inaccurate they were. That's called voter suppression."

"An incredible day. And last night, the Republican Party defied history to expand our Senate majority while significantly beating expectations in the House for the midtown and midterm year.

"Our Second Amendment, which, believe me, is under siege. Our Second Amendment. Our Second Amendment. If Stacey Abrams gets in, your Second Amendment is, is gone, gone. Stacey and her friends will get rid of it. You wouldn't mind if somebody comes knocking on your door, 'Please, I'd like to have your guns turned over to government.' Take your guns away. Please give us all guns right now."

"A highway that would take 20 years to get approved. We go through a process. You believe an environmental impact process, I know it well, would take 20 years, 18 years, 15 years, 22 years. We have it down to two and a half years. We want to get it down to one and a half maybe even one. And by the way, we may reject it if it's not good but you're not going to devote an entire lifetime and then find out at the end it's not going to be approved. And it's going to end up costing 10 times or 20 times more which we have many examples, then it was supposed to. So we have it down really good but we're going to get it down even lower. And again, if it doesn't pass environmental standards, if we do anything to interfere with our clean air or our crystal clean, beautiful water, we won't approve it. Not going to be approved. But we're going to know. We don't have to take 20 years to tell you that do we?"

"Oh, they're going crazy over the nice, beautiful, clean coal. And the beautiful thing is, if we have a national emergency, if we have a problem, big problem, there's nothing like coal. You'll truck that stuff around. If the roads aren't there, you'll turn it around and go through a tree. Those windmills -- number one, when the wind doesn't blow, they tend not to do too well. Right? They tend not to do too well, and they're extremely costly, and they need subsidy. We're paying massive subsidy. And of course, they kill all the birds, you know. Other than that, they're wonderful. No, they don't work too well in times of national emergency. We say, 'We need more energy, but the wind isn't blowing.' One thing with coal: that sucker, you just keep piling it in there, right? Right? Those miners. The miners knew what they were doing. And I don't want to speak badly about natural gas, because I know it. But they drop a little something on one of those pipelines -- that's the end of the natural gas, right? But the coal just keeps coming."

"Anybody throwing stones, rocks -- like they did to Mexico and the Mexican military, Mexican police, where they badly hurt police and soldiers of Mexico -- we will consider that a firearm. Because there's not much difference, where you get hit in the face with a rock -- which, as you know, it was very violent a few days ago -- very, very violent -- that break-in. It was a break-in of a country. They broke into Mexico." And: "There's nothing political about a caravan of thousands of people, and now others forming, pouring up into our country. We have no idea who they are. All we know is they're pretty tough people when they can blast through the Mexican military and Mexican police. They're pretty tough people. Even Mexico said, 'Wow, these are tough people.' I don't want them in our country. And women don't want them in our country." And: "We will consider that the maximum that we can consider that, because they're throwing rocks viciously and violently. You saw that three days ago. Really hurting the military. We're not going to put up with that. If they want to throw rocks at our military, our military fights back. We're going to consider -- and I told them, consider it a rifle. When they throw rocks like they did at the Mexico military and police, I say, consider it a rifle."

"If you want your Stocks to go down, I strongly suggest voting Democrat. They like the Venezuela financial model, High Taxes & Open Borders!"

"But we can't allow people like this (the Pittsburgh synagogue murderer) to become important. And when we change all of our lives in order to accommodate them, it's not acceptable. So I thought of it for a little while, and the press said, are you going to cancel these two events? And frankly, the Future Farmers, I could have done that one. But this is a rally for Mike Bost, and frankly this one maybe I could have, except I don't want to change our life for somebody that's sick and evil. And I don't think we ever should. I don't think we ever should. Remember the New York Stock Exchange. Remember the teams, the Yankees, George Steinbrenner. He said we've got to play, even if nobody comes, if nobody shows up, we got to play. And I remember that George was a tough man. He was a friend of mine. But he was a good man. And he said we got to play. And they all played."

"You see what's going on in California. He (Democratic governor candidate Gavin Newsom) wants to have open borders and everybody worldwide can pour into California, just pour in. And he's going to give you health care and education. You know what? That will be -- I think California will end up being larger than the United States. The whole world is going to come. It's really bad stuff." - Rally 10-26-18

"Literally, people thought -- they love him, and that'll never happen again. I mean, he still won by a lot. But a lot of people didn't vote for a man named Ralph Norman, who's fantastic. Ralph, wherever you are, Ralph? Ralph, right, Ralph? Remember I called you? I said, Ralph, never be so far in front that they don't want to vote, OK? Never let that happen. You're always one point down the next time, Ralph. Thank you, Ralph. Great job. And, Ralph, I'll tell you, he's done a great job. We're also thrilled to be joined by a North Carolina native, because I love NASCAR. Do we like NASCAR? I love NASCAR. And I really love -- you know what I'm talking about -- the France family and Brian France. The Democrats are obstructionists. It's horrible what they're doing. They're not approving people."

"You know we call him Doc Ronny, we call him Admiral Ronny.
Doc, you run a great operation. How do you think you'd do at the VA?"

"I'm really proud of the job we've done for the VA because we got- we're working right now on choice and really big-but we got rid of so many rules and regulations that made it impossible and we're really doing great at the VA."

"I've take the position- and I don't have to take this position and maybe I'll change- that I will not be involved with the Justice Department. I will wait until this is over."

"A horrible thing and yet, I've accomplished, with all of this going on, more than any president in the first year in our history. Even the enemies and the haters admit that."

About Scott Pruitt:
"Scott's done a fantastic job at EPA— I'm not happy about certain things."

To a rally in Minnesota:

"Hispanic American unemployment has reached its lowest level ever recorded the history our country. And remember, I'd go into big stadiums like this that were packed?
And by the way, you're very good at real estate. Did you see the thousands and thousands of people outside?
And I usually go home my wife would say "How was the crowd?" Although honestly, when you have many thousands of people like have tonight- you know, I was at an event three weeks ago where a person from the New York Times said, "There was only a thousand people."

"And we all have ego, but I don't want to show my face."

"I want to show the crowds. It's much prettier. Because you people are incredible. Unemployment among women has reach the lowest level as of today in 65 years."

"But I'll tell you, to keep this incredible momentum, I think maybe the most successful that the country has ever had.
In 500 days, we've cut more regulations than any president in the history of our country, whether it's four years, eight years, or in one year - in one case, 16 years."

"We were going in for a routine repeal and replace, and he went thumbs down. Not nice. That was not nice."

"And together, we will make America wealthy again."

About Sen. Dean Heller at a rally:
"We started out, we weren't friends. I didn't like him. He didn't like me."

"I mean Wacky Jacky will never vote for us, folks. Never. She's wacky. She's never going to vote for us."

"Hey! I'm the President* of the United States! I'm not the president* of the globe."

"I want to give a victory speech."

"Hispanic, any Hispanic here? I think so. Any Asians? Asian? Asian? Any Asian?"

"Look, I'm 48 and 1 in the primaries, and actually it's much higher than that because I endorsed a lot of people that were successful that people don't even talk about."

About 2020 presidential possibilities
"I see no talent."

Montana rally Oct. 19, 2018:
"That was one of those quickies. I love those states. You know, the polls close. Polls have just closed in the state of Montana. Trump has won Montana."

"We like the-we like the- it's just a flowing. They do comma. They don't do- they do a comma."

"This will be an election of Kavanaugh, the caravan, law and order, and common sense."

"It's incredible the deep state where they don't even look at her. Isn't it incredible? (about Hillary?)

But I like acid-washing, because that really says it. She acid-washes 33,000, so that nobody can ever find-but they're around some place. I think that maybe- maybe they're at the State Department. But maybe they're at the State Department. They could very well be at the Department of Justice, if you can believe that whole deal. But we're just being quiet. We're being quiet. Do you know why? There's been no collusion. If I ever called the Russians, the first one to know about it would be the state of Montana, and they wouldn't be too happy. Can you imagine? Let's call the Russians? It's a disgrace."

"Barbara Walters interviewed me. Do you mind if I play with your hair? Do you remember that? And then numerous people have done that. But that's ok. But the choice could not be more clear. Democrats produce mobs. Republicans produce jobs."

"Democrats have become the party of crime. It's true.
I said, I'm gong to put that in. I'm going to say that when I make speeches. Nobody's ever challenged it. Maybe they have. Who knows? I have to always say that, because then they'll say they did actually challenge it, and they'll put like- then they'll say he gets a Pinocchio.
But Greg is smart. And by the way, never wrestle him. You understand that? Never. Any guy that can do a body slam, he's my kind of.. he was my guy.
But I've done so many campaign - I'm so far ahead. But- but we've started the wall. And it's moving. And we're going to get it, but get me some republican votes, please."

"We need a great president."

About working on a tax cut
"So the Republican Party has various groups, all great people. They're great people. But some are moderate, some are very conservative. The Democrats don't seem to have that nearly as much. You know the Democrats have, they don't have that. The Republicans do have that. And I think it's fine. But you know there's a pretty vast area in there. And I have a great relationship with all of them. Now, we have government not closing. I think we'll be in great shape on that. It's going very well. Obviously, that takes precedent."

About the first 100 days:
AP: Can I ask you, over your first 100 days — you're not quite there yet — how do you feel like the office has changed you?

TRUMP: Well the one thing I would say — and I say this to people — I never realized how big it was. Everything's so (unintelligible) like, you know the orders are so massive. I was talking to —

AP: You mean the responsibility of it, or do you mean —

TRUMP: Number One, there's great responsibility. When it came time to, as an example, send out the 59 missiles, the Tomahawks in Syria. I'm saying to myself, "You know, this is more than just like, 79 (sic) missiles. This is death that's involved," because people could have been killed. This is risk that's involved, because if the missile goes off and goes in a city or goes in a civilian area — you know, the boats were hundreds of miles away — and if this missile goes off and lands in the middle of a town or a hamlet .... every decision is much harder than you'd normally make. (unintelligible) ...

This is involving death and life and so many things. ... So it's far more responsibility. (unintelligible) ....The financial cost of everything is so massive, every agency. This is thousands of times bigger, the United States, than the biggest company in the world. The second-largest company in the world is the Defense Department. The third-largest company in the world is Social Security. The fourth-largest — you know, you go down the list.

AP: Right.

TRUMP. It's massive. And every agency is, like, bigger than any company. So you know, I really just see the bigness of it all, but also the responsibility. And the human responsibility. You know, the human life that's involved in some of the decisions.

They had a quote from me that NATO's obsolete. But they didn't say why it was obsolete. I was on Wolf Blitzer, very fair interview, the first time I was ever asked about NATO, because I wasn't in government. People don't go around asking about NATO if I'm building a building in Manhattan, right? So they asked me, Wolf ... asked me about NATO, and I said two things. NATO's obsolete — not knowing much about NATO, now I know a lot about NATO — NATO is obsolete, and I said, "And the reason it's obsolete is because of the fact they don't focus on terrorism." You know, back when they did NATO there was no such thing as terrorism.

He was asked about the dreamers and DACA:
"No, we aren't looking to do anything right now. Look, the dreamers ... this is an interesting case, they left and they came back and he's got some problems, it's a little different than the dreamer case, right? But we are putting MS-13 in jail and getting them the hell out of our country. They've taken over

towns and cities and we are being really brutal with MS-13, and that's what we should be. They are a bad group, and somebody said they are as bad as al-Qaida, which is a hell of a reference. So we are moving criminals out of our country and we are getting them out in record numbers and those are the people we are after. We are not after the dreamers, we are after the criminals."

About Beto O'Rourke:
"I thought you were supposed to win before you run for president."

"And then I flew to Iraq; first time I left the White House -- because I stayed in the White House for months and months because I wanted the Democrats to get back from their vacations from Hawaii and these other places. And I figured it would look good if I stayed in the White House so that you people all love me and vote for me, okay? I figured it would look good. I figured it would look good. So I stayed in the White House...I stayed for Thanksgiving. I said -- I mean, I was in the White House for a long time. Months. Months. I had cabin fever in the White House. But if you've got to have cabin fever, that's the place to do it, okay? But I was there, I don't know, for a number of months, through Christmas."
And: "But I sat in the White House for months and months, except I took a day off."

To Sean Hannity:
"It's so ridiculous (the Green New Deal). No planes, let's not fly anymore. It is crazy. But personally, they should go for it. I love it."

To Governors:

"And in China, they have a very, very tough penalty for drugs. It's called the death penalty. And I said to President Xi, 'You don't have much of a drug problem. Do you have a drug problem?'' 'No. No drug problem.' I said, 'So you have 1.4 billion people, and you don't have a drug problem?' 'That's right. No drug problem.' I said, 'What do you attribute that to?' 'Death penalty. Quick trial.' They don't have trials that last 19 years. At the end of a -- the judge dies. Everybody dies. The only one living is the one that did the damage. No, they have what's called a 'quick trial.' It goes quick. It doesn't take a lot of time. And if you're a drug dealer, you'll say, 'You know what -- maybe I'll just sort of stay out of China.' Singapore, the same thing."

"Well, I condemn any election fraud. And when I look at what's happened in California with the votes, when I look at what happened -- as you know, there was just a case where they found a million fraudulent votes." And: " I condemn any voter fraud of any kind, whether it's Democrat or Republican -- or when you look at some of the things that happened in California, in particular."

"And then you have the lottery. It's a horror show, because when countries put people into the lottery, they're not putting you in; they're putting some very bad people in the lottery. It's common sense. If I ran a country, and if I have a lottery system of people going to the United States, I'm not going to put in my stars; I'm going to put in people I don't want. The lottery system is a disaster. I'm stuck with it."

"The Democrats in Congress don't want to touch any of it. Visa lottery -- that's where they put in the names; they put it in a lottery, and you pick, 'Oh, here's a wonderful

person. Wonderful. You know, he killed four people.'
'Here's -- here's another wonderful.' And then they get in and
we say, 'Gee, that person just came into our country. He just
robbed a store and killed somebody.' How is that possible?
Because they send us the people they don't want."

"But the governor (of Virginia) stated that he would even
allow a newborn baby to come out into the world and wrap
the baby and make the baby comfortable. And then talk to the
mother and talk to the father and then execute the baby.
Execute the baby. Incredible."

"I have intel people, but that doesn't mean I have to agree.
President Bush had intel people that said Saddam Hussein in
Iraq had nuclear weapons -- had all sorts of weapons of mass
destruction. Guess what? Those intel people didn't know what
the hell they were doing, and they got us tied up in a war that
we should have never been in. And we've spent $7 trillion in
the Middle East and we have lost lives…"

"The Democrats went out and said 'Awww- they should've
done better.'
So what I'm thinking of doing - getting Chuck Schumer-
getting Nancy Pelosi- having them bring two or three of their
brilliant representatives, and we'll all go down together. What
we'll do is we'll negotiate- I'll put them in the room, and let
them speak up. Because any deal I make with China it's
gonna be better than any deal anyone ever dreamt possible.
Or, I'm not gonna have a deal. Very simple."

About voter fraud:
"This is a problem in California that's so bad of illegals
voting. This is a California problem, and if you notice, almost

every race — I was watching today — out of, like, 11 races that are in question, they're gonna win all of them.
The Republicans don't win, and that's because of potentially illegal votes, which is what I've been saying for a long time. I have no doubt about it. And I've seen it, I've had friends talk about it when people get in line that have absolutely no right to vote and they go around in circles. Sometimes they go to their car, put on a different hat, put on a different shirt, come in and vote again. Nobody takes anything. It's really a disgrace what's going on."

"The disgrace is that, voter ID. If you buy, you know, a box of cereal, if you do anything, you have a voter ID."

"If you look at what happened in New Hampshire, where thousands of people came up and voted from a very liberal part of Massachusetts and they came up in buses and they voted. I said, "What's going on over here"; my people said, "You won New Hampshire easily except they have tremendous numbers of buses coming up." They're pouring up by the hundreds, buses of people getting out, voting. Then they're supposed to go back within 90 days. And of the people that are supposed to go back, almost none of them do. In other words, they go back after the vote is over. They go back — and I think it's like 3 percent — I mean, almost nobody goes back to show that, you know, that they were allowed to vote. And so what do you do? Recall the election. Recall the election. I mean, there, you should be able to recall the election."

Kellyanne Conway then contributes:
TRUMP: Had I not been winning Florida by more than they could — I mean, you can't produce — if you have a million

people, you can't give 1,200,000 votes, okay? So actually, what happened is they went with fairly accurate numbers because whether I won by 10 votes or by half a million votes, it didn't matter. But I had, fortunately, enough votes, and they were sitting there waiting. They said, "Broward County is not reporting." This went on for hours.

CONWAY: The Panhandle came in an hour later.

TRUMP: Well, the Panhandle was so devastating to Crooked Hillary, that, frankly, it didn't make any difference, okay? Because the Panhandle was so — it was, like, 98 percent. That thing came in, then all of a sudden Broward came in. And I won by, you know, I won by a lot of votes. I call it four Yankee Stadiums.

About Brian Kemp's victory in Georgia:
"It was 70-30, something like that, 70-30 or 70-40, maybe 70-40. But it was an easy win."

"Congratulations. Congratulations, Mississippi."

"And Republicans will always protect Americans with pre-existing conditions.
So, the wall has started, very, very substantially."
"Now they call me a politician. I'm a politician. I can't stand it. They said he's a political person. But I've only had one race, and look at the result. You know that. You know that. You know that. You know what I'm talking about."

"I have absolute right to do what I want to do with the Justice Department."

"How is everything in Florida doing? Ok? Weather's good? Right? It's Florida- welcome to the southern White House. The border's coming along very well, it's become very strong. We're getting some terrible decisions from the 9th Circuit as usual.

We are doing really well considering the laws are a disaster. If we had the right laws it would be a lot less expensive and we'd do it a lot easier. But we don't have the right laws and we have people interpreting the laws and they always give us a bad interpretation."

"Even our legislation that we passed- it failed in the 9th Circuit, it failed in the 9th Circuit appeal then it won in the Supreme Court. And it's just a shame because it's really hurting people. It's hurting our law enforcement tremendously, and now that the military's on the border it's really hurting our military. And frankly when they hear these decisions these are professionals the military the law enforcement the first responders- they can't believe the decisions that are being made by these judges. This is what they do , they do law enforcement law and order and they get these decisions and they say who makes these decisions? They're not into lawyer things."

"Well, it's one plant in Ohio. But I love Ohio. And I told them: You're playing around with the wrong person. And Ohio wasn't properly represented by their Democrat senator, Senator Brown, because he didn't get the point across. But we will all together get the point across to General Motors. And they better damn well open up a new plant there very quickly. You know, they haven't closed — they're reallocating it, it's called. And I said, because their Cruze car isn't selling, OK? They make a car called Chevy Cruze. And it's not selling well. So I said: Then put a car that is selling well in there but get it open fast."

"What would be a fair deal with Europe?
A fair deal is that they have to take down their barriers and that they have to start — stop charging us massive taxes for our people — and also their standards. For instance, they'll create a standard — we'll make a product, and they'll make a standard that's different than the product, lower or higher. But it's different. So then our product can't come into the EU. They do that all the time, like with medical equipment, OK? But they have to take down their barriers and they have to take off the taxes. And, frankly, they have to start treating our companies better, because they sue all of our companies for billions and billions of dollars. They're picking up all this money from our companies. We should be the ones to sue our companies."

From Washington Post interview 11/27/18:
"And I'm not blaming anybody, but I'm just telling you I think that the Fed is way off-base with what they're doing, number one. Number two, a positive note, we're doing very well on trade, we're doing very well — our companies are very strong. Don't forget we're still up from when I came in 38 percent or something. You know, it's a tremendous — it's not like we're up — and we're much stronger. And we're much more liquid. And the banks are now much more liquid during my tenure. And I'm not doing – I'm not playing by the same rules as Obama. Obama had zero interest to worry about; we're paying interest, a lot of interest. He wasn't paying down — we're talking about $50 billion lots of different times, paying down and knocking out liquidity. Well, Obama didn't do that. And just so you understand, I'm

playing a normalization economy whereas he's playing a free economy. It's easy to make money when you're paying no interest. It's easy to make money when you're not doing any pay-downs, so you can't — and despite that, the numbers we have are phenomenal numbers."

"I don't do anything ... just for political gain. But I will tell you, politically speaking, that issue is a total winner. People look at the border, they look at the rush to the police, they look at the rock throwers and really hurting three people, three very brave Border Patrol folks — I think that it's a tremendous issue, but much more importantly, is really needed. So we have to have border security."

The famous Lester Holt interview in May 2017:
"He [Rod Rosenstein] made a recommendation, he's highly respected, very good guy, very smart guy. The Democrats like him, the Republicans like him. He made a recommendation. But regardless of [the] recommendation, I was going to fire Comey. Knowing there was no good time to do it!"

"And the reason they should've won it is, the Electoral College is almost impossible for a Republican to win, it's very hard, because you start off at such a disadvantage. So everybody was thinking they should have won the election. This was an excuse for having lost an election."

"And this group of major losers did not just ruthlessly attack me, my family and everyone who questioned their lies they tried to divide our country.
They did it all because they refused to accept the results of one of the greatest presidential elections, probably number one, in our history."

"Little pencil neck Adam Schiff ... got the smallest, thinnest neck I've ever seen. He is not a long ball hitter."

"I would like to promise and pledge to all of my voters and supporters and to all of the people of the United States that I will totally accept the results of this great and historic presidential election— if I win,"

"And our friends, Tucker, Sean, Laura, through the roof last night.
Then it comes to a place called Michigan. Have you ever heard of Michigan?
And I remember leaving and I said, so [Hillary Clinton's] got 500 people and I had 32,000 people including the people outside.I will tell you, we have more tonight because outside we have even more than we did then.
She has 500 or 600 people, I have 32,000.
We won, we won a lot. We won a lot. Well, we won 306 to 223. Would you say that's good? I'd say it is.
Red was killing -- they were dying.
They came from the valleys. They came from the mountains. They came out of the damn rivers.
I don't know what you were doing in the river but they came from the cities."

"The Democrats have to now decide whether they will continue defrauding the public with ridiculous bullshit."

"We did great with women and I think we're going to do better with women now."

"And we believe in the words and always will we're not changing it. They want us to change a lot of things. It's not happening. Of our national motto, 'In God We Trust', 'In God We Trust'."

Declaring national emergency:
"So, I'm going to be signing a national emergency, it's been signed many times before. Something signed many times, many, many times, by other presidents."

"I expect to be sued. I shouldn't be sued. Very rarely do you get sued when you do a national emergency. And then other people say 'Well, if you use it for this' well what are we using it for?…we've gotta get rid of drugs and gangs and people - it's an invasion! We have an invasion of drugs and criminals coming into our country. That we stop. But it's very hard to stop. With a wall it would be very easy… Sadly, we'll be sued. Sadly we'll go through a process and happily we'll win. I think."

"We will have a national emergency, and we will then be sued, and they will sue us in the 9th Circuit, even though it shouldn't be there, and we will possibly get a bad ruling, and then we will get another bad ruling, and then we will end up in the Supreme Court."

"I went through Congress. I made a deal. I got $1.4 billion when I wasn't supposed to get one dollar. Not one dollar. He's not going to get one dollar. Well I got $1.4 billion but I'm not happy with it. I also got billions and billions of dollars for other things- port of entries lots of other things - the purchase of drug equipment- more than we were even requesting. In fact the primary fight was on the wall- everything else we have so much, as I said, I don't know what to do with it we have so much money. But on the wall, they skimped. So I was successful in that sense, but I want to do it faster. I could do the wall over a longer period of time. I didn't need to do this, but I'd rather do it much faster."

"I just want to get it done faster. That's all."

"I can tell you I have the support of the police, the support of the military, the support of the bikers for Trump- I have the tough people, but they don't play it tough- until they go to a certain point, and then it would be bad, very bad."

"We have to get a win or I'll have to go national security, one or the other."

About Comey's memos:
"He does these memos and then fake news CNN who's a total fake- you know, they give Hillary Clinton the questions to the debate and nobody - can you imagine, by the way, if you gave me the questions to a debate?"

Tweeted 2/24/19:

HOLD THE DATE! We will be having one of the biggest gatherings in the history of Washington, D.C., on July 4th. It will be called "A Salute To America" and will be held at the Lincoln Memorial. Major fireworks display, entertainment and an address by your favorite President*, me!

July 23, 2019
To students
"Then, I have an Article II, where I have to the right to do whatever I want as president*. But I don't even talk about that."

Business Acumen

(The business genius at work…I wonder what we could learn from his taxes.)

"The first thing the secretary types is the boss."

"Money was never a big motivation for me, except as a way to keep score. The real excitement is playing the game."

March 2011 on the phone w Fox & Friends:
"I dealt with Qaddafi. I rented him a piece of land. He paid me more for one night than the land was worth for two years, and then I didn't let him use the land. That's what we should be doing. I don't want to use the word 'screwed', but I screwed him. That's what we should be doing."

"Remember the $5 billion website? I hire people, they do a web site. It costs me $3.00"

"They drafted him (Babe Ruth). They took him as a pitcher, but they knew they wanted to make him a hitter."

"Babe Ruth was one of the best pitchers. He still has records today. In 1920, he started with the New York Yankees. And I have heard for many years -- what's the worst trade in the history of sports? Babe Ruth, 19-year-old pitcher, for $100,000 and a 35-year-old third baseman. That was not a good trade -- who was out of baseball the following season. That was not good. Of course, $100,000 is probably like $25 million today, but it was still a lousy deal."

"You take a look at soybeans, if you go back five years from when I won from the election, they cut in half. They were literally cut it in half, meaning they went down in half."

"Chrysler is coming back. Chrysler just announced they're coming back."

"We're the piggy bank that everybody was robbing for 30 years."

"Nike is a tenant of mine. They pay a lot of rent."
(about the ad campaign with Colin Kaepernick)

Tweets:
1/4/18 Dow just crashes through 25,000. Congrats!
7/14/18 The stock market hit 25,000 yesterday. It's all happening!
1/30/19 Dow just broke 25,000. Tremendous news!

"In real life, if I were firing you, I'd tell you what a great job you did, how fantastic you are, and how you can do better someplace else. If somebody steals, that's different, but generally speaking, you want to let them down as lightly as possible. It's not a very pleasant thing. I don't like firing people."

"The way I run my business seems to be easier than the way I run my life."

"We're going to be opening up the labor forces because we have to. We have so many companies coming in. People like Tim — you're expanding all over and doing things that I really wanted you to do right from the beginning. I used to say, 'Tim, you gotta start doing it here,' and you really have you've really put a big investment in our country. We appreciate it very much, Tim Apple."

Interview with NYTimes 7-20-17:
"Because you are basically saying from the moment the insurance, you're 21 years old, you start working and you're paying $12 a year for insurance, and by the time you're 70, you get a nice plan. Here's something where you walk up and say, 'I want my insurance'."

"Insurance is, you're 20 years old, you just graduated from college, and you start paying $15 a month for the rest of your life and by the time you're 70, and you really need it, you're still paying the same amount and that's really insurance."

Interview w Sean Hannity 10/17:
"I'm so proud of the $5.2 trillion dollars of increase in the stock market. Now, if you look at the stock market, that's one element, but then we have many other elements. The country — we took it over, it owed $20 trillion, as you know, the last eight years they borrowed more than it did in the whole history of our country, so they borrowed more than $10 trillion — and yet, we

picked up $5.2 trillion in the stock market, possibly picked up the whole things in terms of the first nine months in terms of value. So, you could say in one sense we are really increasing values, and maybe in a sense we are reducing debt."

"My daughter, Ivanka, who is going to be speaking later, is -- she has been so much involved. So incredibly involved. Where is Ivanka? Ivanka, keep -- keep going. Created -- my daughter has created millions of jobs. I don't know if anyone knows that, but she's created millions of jobs..."

"And we have companies opening up in the United States that we thought we lost, that would never be back, and some are coming back and some are brand new and they're big. And they're coming in and they're moving in, which is one of the reasons we need people to come in. They have to come in through a legal process. But with a 3.7 [per cent] unemployment, we need to have people coming in."

"So, I love tariffs, but I also love them to negotiate."

They failed on the Mueller Report, they failed on Robert Mueller's testimony, they failed on everything else, so now the Democrats are trying to build a case that I enrich myself by being President*. Good idea, except I will, and have always expected to, lose BILLIONS of DOLLARS..for the privilege of being your President* - and doing the best job that has been done in many decades. I am far beyond somebody paying for a hotel room for the evening, or filling up a gas tank at an airport I do not own. These Radical Left Democrats are CRAZY! Obama Netflix?

Random Bits and Things We Did Not Know

(When I do a word search for the "wisdom", it only appears one time in this whole document, and it wasn't used by DJT)

"Do you mind if I sit back a little? Because your breath is very bad."

"Private jets cost a lot of money."

"Owning a great golf course gives you great power."

"The 1990's sure aren't like the 1980's."

"Poverty is plummeting."

"It's a big monster."

"I have known Kanye a little bit and I get along with Kanye. I get along with a lot of people, frankly."

"We like the-we like the- it's just a flowing. They do comma. They don't do- they do a comma."

"Well, it's big sky. I guess there's a reason for everything, right? no, it's just - I got out and I'm looking- I've been here many times— but I got out and I'm looking- I say, that really is big sky."

"Sting. Sting would be another person who's a hero. The must that he's created over the years. I don't really listen to it, but the fact that he's making it, I respect that."

On being at the White House on Christmas:
"I was here on Christmas evening, I was all by myself in the White House. That's a big, big house. Except for all the guys out on the lawn with machine guns… I was waving to them. I never saw so many guys with machine guns in my life. Secret Service and military. These are great people.They don't play games. They don't like wave. They don't even smile. But I was there all alone with the machine gunners. I felt very safe. I have to tell you. Great people. There's a lot of them. But I was hoping that maybe somebody would come back and negotiate."

"I don't like losers."

"My whole life is about winning. I don't lose often. I almost never lose."

"I actually don't have a bad hairline."

"People love me. And you know what, I have been very successful. Everybody loves me."

"You know that ISIS wants to go in and take over the Vatican? You have heard that. You know, that's a dream of theirs, to go in to Italy."

Other things we didn't know:

"People don't realize. You know, if you go back to the Civil War, it was the Republicans that really did the thing."

"People don't realize we are an unbelievably divided country."

"People don't know this about Iraq, but the among the largest oil reserves in the world."

"De-nuclearization is a very important- it's a very important word-become a very well used word-and a lot of people don't know what it means."

"People don't realize what a big country Mexico is."

"You know, people don't understand. I went to an Ivy League college- I was a nice student-I did very well-I'm a very intelligent person-"

"We have steel mills being built all over the country. Nobody saw anything like it ever before."

"They can dump all they want. I want them to dump a lot."

"But we're making a lot of money. We're making a lot of money."

"They want to dump, it's ok. Dump all you want."

"It's called the USMCA, like the song, YMCA, right?"

"It's called the Space Force. Very important. Very, very important."
"We want to get to that 53 number. They don't believe it, but they don't want to talk about it, but that's ok."

"This is the one we want. We want ourselves. We want us and that's what we got."

"If Romney fought as hard against Obama as he does me, he'd be president."

"Go get yourself a good socialist."

"A certificate of live birth is not the same thing by any stretch of the imagination as a birth certificate."

"I have great respect for the U.K. United Kingdom. Great respect. Some people all it Britain. They call it Great Britain. They used to call it England. Different parts."

"I miss the name England. You don't hear the name England as much as you should. You understand that? I think England is a beautiful name. People call it Britain. They call it Great Britain. They used to call it England."

About daughter Ivanka's project:

"She's so formal! A special person, she's worked so hard as you all know. And I want to thank you Ivanka, for your devotion to the America workers-our great workers- and nobody has workers like we do. So I just want to thank you, HONEY, great job."

"You've worked so hard on the kidney. Very special ... the kidney has a very special place in the heart."

From Roger Stone's book *Clinton's War on Women*
"The one time I visited [Epstein's] Palm Beach home, the swimming pool was full of beautiful young girls. 'How nice,' I thought, 'he let the neighborhood kids use his pool.' "

"Can you believe that, with all of the problems and difficulties facing the U.S., President Obama spent the day playing golf. Worse than Carter,"

To a rally in Feb. 2016:
"I love golf, but if I were in the White House, I don't think I'd ever see Turnberry again. I don't think I'd ever see Doral again.I don't ever think I'd see anything. I just want to stay in the White House and work my ass off."

Philosophy of Life

(Another window into the mystery that is Donald J. Trump. Shouldn't we all live by these principles..?)

With Rona Barrett:
"I think my philosophy basically is there has to be something to this. I mean we just can't be put here for the sake of living our 60, 70, 80, 90, 100 years, whatever it might be, and just end up with nothing at the end of that time after all the combat, and I really look at life to a certain extent as combat. There has to be something. I mean we have to be in a test period or there has to be something after this. Otherwise, it just seems so futile."

"The point is that you can't be too greedy." (I think he means that there's no such thing as too much greed?)

"I apologize when I'm wrong." (Hahahahahahah)

"I think apologizing's a great thing, but you have to be wrong. I will absolutely apologize, sometime in the hopefully distant future, if I'm ever wrong."

May 2011 New York Times interview:
"It's like in golf. A lot of people -- I don't want this to sound trivial -- but a lot of people are switching to these really long putters, very unattractive. It's weird. You see these great players with these really long putters, because they can't sink three-footers anymore. And, I hate it. I am a traditionalist. I have so many fabulous friends who happen to be gay, but I am a traditionalist."

"Well, I read a lot … and over my life, I've read so much." (The Hugh Hewitt Show, February 25, 2015)

"I don't read much. Mostly I read contracts, but usually my lawyers do most of the work. There are too many pages." (Veja, February 2014)

"Believe it or not, even when I'm in Washington or New York, I do not watch much television."

"I don't have a lot of time for listening to television." (New York Times, July 28, 2015)

"I actually love watching television." (The Hugh Hewitt Show, February 25, 2015)

"The day I realized it can be smart to be shallow was, for me, a deep experience." (Trump: Think Like a Billionaire, 2004)

"I don't mind being criticized. I'll never, ever complain." (CNN, September 24, 2015)

"How do you get 100 percent of anything? We always have somebody who says 'I don't like Trump, I don't like our president*, he destroyed my career. I only destroy their career because they said bad things about me and you fight back and they go down the tubes and that's OK."

About his club in Charlotte NC at the time of Hurricane Florence:
"How is Lake Norman doing? I love that area. I can't tell you why, but I love that area.
I actually have investments in Charlotte. They'll say 'oh, that's a conflict of interest.' Fake news, they'll say this is a conflict of interest. You know where my club is, right? Trump National. It's a very big success on Lake Norman. Beautiful. Largest man-made lake in the world by far, right?"

"I don't like losers. My whole life is about winning. I don't lose often. I almost never lose."

"I actually don't have a bad hairline."

"People love me. And you know what, I have been very successful. Everybody loves me."

"I like the idea of amending the 1964 Civil Rights Act to include a ban of discrimination based on sexual orientation. It would be simple. It would be straightforward."

"I'll drink water. Sometimes tomato juice, which I like. Sometimes orange juice, which I like. I'll drink different things. But the Coke or Pepsi boosts you up a little."

"Compromise is in my vocabulary, very strongly."

"The buck stops with everybody."

"The way I run my business seems to be easier than the way I run my life."

10-22-16
"After this election I'm going to sue every liar who said something bad about me. There won't be a newspaper left in this country when I'm through with them. And these lying women, these bimbos, I will destroy them."

About non-violence:

"I'll beat the crap outta you."

"Part of the problem is nobody wants to hurt each other anymore."

"The audience hit back— that's what we need more of."

"Knock the crap outta them."

"I'd like to punch him in the face."

"If you do (hurt him) - I'll defend you in court. Don't worry."

"If she gets to pick her judges, there's nothing you can do... although with the Second amendment people maybe there is..."

"We have a stupid system of courts. It's the craziest thing in the world. We could be the only country that has it. You put a foot on the property, you put a foot into the United States. Congratulations, go get Perry Mason to represent you."

About Jeff Sessions:
"The only reason I gave him the job because I felt loyalty. He was an original supporter. He was on the campaign."

At a Las Vegas rally Sept 2018:
"This is an incredible time for our country. America is winning again."
A few moments later
"It is a pretty sad day, isn't it? Don't worry. It's all going to get better. It's all going to get better."

"The public means the enemy."

Loyalty

(This is just a few of the examples. Dante said "All hope abandon ye who enter here." I think he meant not Hell, but the world of this president*)

"The thing that's most important to me is loyalty. You can't hire loyalty. I've had people over the years who I swore were loyal to me, and it turned out that they weren't. Then I've had people that I didn't have the same confidence in and turned out to be extremely loyal. So you never really know. The thing I really look for though, over the longer term, is loyalty."

About Lev Parnas and Igor Fruman:
"I don't know these gentlemen. It's possible I have a picture with them because I have a picture with everybody, I have a picture with everybody here. But somebody said there may be a picture or something at a fundraiser or somewhere but I have a pictures with everybody. I don't know if there's anybody I don't have a picture with. I don't know about them, I don't know what they do. But I don't know, maybe they were clients of Rudy. You'll have to ask Rudy, I just don't know."

About Ambassador Gordon Sondland:
"I don't know him very well."

About his press secretary Anthony Scaramucci:
"I barely knew him until his 11 days of gross incompetence,"

"Anthony Scaramucci is a highly unstable 'nut job'…, I barely knew him."

About the porn star with whom he had an affair, Stormy Daniels:
"I had nothing to do with her. So she can lie and she can do whatever she wants to do." Also, some time later: "Horseface. She knows nothing about me."

About his aide George Papadopoulos:
"Few people knew the young, low level volunteer named George, who has already proven to be a liar."
And that photo of him seated next to Papadopoulos? "I never even talked to the guy,"

About his campaign manager Paul Manafort:
"I didn't know Manafort well, he wasn't with the campaign long."

About Matthew Whitaker, temporary acting Secretary of Justice:
"I don't know Matt Whitaker."

About George Conway:
"I barely know him, but just take a look, a stone cold LOSER
& husband from hell!"

About his friend Jeffrey Epstein:
"I knew him like everybody in Palm Beach knew him,"
Trump told reporters at the White House. "...He was a fixture
in Palm Beach. I had a falling out with him a long time ago. I
don't think I have spoken with him for 15 years. I was not a
fan."

About rapper Lil'Jon, who was a two-time contestant on The
Apprentice:
"I don't know who Lil Jon is. I don't — I really don't,"

The Media

To Ted Koppel 7-21-16:
"No, the media's been very dishonest, but we put up with it.
But I let people know about it. There's tremendous dishonesty
in the media. But I let people know about it."

"And by the way, some are tremendously honest, but you
have tremendous dishonesty in the media, tremendous. I've
never seen anything like it, more so in the last number of
months, I think, than I've ever seen it. With that being said,
you have to power through it, and I do that. And it seems to
be working out pretty well. But I do like to expose it."

"Well, I think that I'm an honest person. I feel I'm an honest
person. And I don't mind being criticized at all by the media,
but I do wanna -- you know, I do want them to be straight
about it."

"In fact, I hate to say, it was reported this morning, and it was
reported on Fox."

"Another reason that I'm going to win another four years is
because newspapers, television, all forms of media will tank

if I'm not there because without me, their ratings are going down the tubes.
So they basically have to let me win."

"And by the way, NBC may be -- NBC may be the most dishonest reporters of all time."

"And I'd say 80% of you are possibly in coordination with the opposition party."
She's being protected by the fake news back there. Boy, that's a lot -- look at all the people. It's like the Academy Awards -- look at this. That's a lot of stuff. You think this happens to the average president? No way. And every single time, I hope you're enjoying yourselves. You can turn the cameras back on them. I won't say anything bad, I promise. Now, when they think I'm ready to say something bad, all those red lights go off."

"See this, there's the fake news media, they do a lot of -- they do a lot of -- they do a lot phony polls. They do a lot of phony polls, they do a lot of polls, they call them suppression polls, they make a bad -- although our polls now are good, they're good because we're doing a lot of good work, but they make them bad, so you go to a movie instead of voting, you say: 'Well, you know, Alice, let's go to a movie, then we'll come home and watch the returns'."

About CNN:
"I don't watch them at all."
"I watched last night."
"You know, one of the reasons people say you're still looking good, Mr. President. How do you do it?"

"I have an ability- I don't watch NBC anymore. They're as bad as CNN."

"I don't watch things now."

"I did watch a liar-leaker and his performance, by the way, was horrible."

To the Daily Caller 11/15/18

"Because with the fake news, if you tell a joke, if you're sarcastic, if you're having fun with the audience, if you're on live television with millions of people and 25,000 people in an arena, and if you say something like, 'Russia, please, if you can, get us Hillary Clinton's emails. Please, Russia, please. Please get us the emails. Please!'" (Crowd chants "Lock her up!") "So everybody is having a good time. I'm laughin', we're all havin' fun. And then that fake CNN and others say, 'He asked Russia to go get the emails. Horrible.' I mean, I saw it -- like, two weeks ago, I'm watching and they're talking about one of the points. 'He asked Russia for the emails.' These people are sick. And I'm telling you, they know the game. They know the game, and they play it dirty, dirtier than anybody has ever played the game. Dirtier than it's ever been played."

About CNN:

"Now they get it, and you know they had a very high approval rating before I became president*, and I think it's actually a great achievement of mine. Their approval rating now is down as low as just about anybody. And much lower than your president*. I actually have good approval ratings, which nobody ever writes. I was at 51, I guess, with Rasmussen the other day.

Well, I think they behaved badly. I remember Sam Donaldson was terrible at two presidents, and, you know, we tend to forget. I think that now it's become, with cable television playing such a role, although, you know, cable television was supposed to be a dying medium. And because of me, it's now hotter than it's ever been. But someday I won't be here and it will die like you've never seen."

About Jim Acosta:
"He was very rude to the young lady. I won't, I won't even- who knows. Who knows."

"Go ahead, ABC - not NBC. I like ABC a little bit more, not much. Come on ABC- not much, pretty close."

"I'm a believer in the polls, by the way. Rarely do you see a poll that's very far off."

REPORTER: If I could just actually ask that question, Mr. Trump. You didn't let me ask my question.
TRUMP: You've been asking a question for ten minutes. Please sit down. Please, go ahead. Go ahead.

9-27-19
Tweet
To show you how dishonest the LameStream Media is, I used the word Liddle', not Liddle, in discribing Corrupt Congressman Liddle' Adam Schiff. Low ratings @CNN purposely took the hyphen out and said I spelled the word little wrong. A small but never ending situation with CNN!

"The fake news, of which many of you are members, is trying to convince the public to have a recession. 'Let's have a recession'".

Modesty and Humility

(It's not coincidence I don't think, that this is one of the longer chapters. I'm sure he's trying to convince us.)

"I called it."

"I know more about the big bills ... [Inaudible] ... than any president* that's ever been in office."

"I know the details of taxes better than anybody. Better than the greatest CPA."

On the Jimmy Fallon show 9/2015:
"I think apologizing's a great thing, but you have to be wrong. I will absolutely apologize, sometime in the hopefully distant future, if I'm ever wrong."

In his book Surviving at the top:
"I've never had any trouble in bed, but if I'd had affairs with half the starlets and female athletes the newspapers linked me with, I'd have no time to breathe."

"I think the only difference between me and the other candidates is that I'm more honest and my women are more beautiful."

Considering entering the 2012 race, on GMA:
"Part of the beauty of me is that I am very rich."

How to Get Rich 2004:
"Fortunately, I don't pride myself on being a know-it-all."

"I'm a thinker, and I have been a thinker. ... I'm a very deep thinker." (Palm Beach, Florida, March 11, 2016)

"I don't mind being criticized. I'll never, ever complain." (CNN, September 24, 2015)

"I avoid people with especially high opinions of their own abilities or worth." (Trump: Think Big, 2007)

In an interview with The Economist:

TRUMP: We have to prime the pump.
ECONOMIST: It's very Keynesian.
TRUMP: We're the highest-taxed nation in the world. Have you heard that expression before, for this particular type of an event?
ECONOMIST: Priming the pump?
TRUMP: Yeah, have you heard it?
ECONOMIST: Yes.

TRUMP: Have you heard that expression used before? Because I haven't heard it. I mean, I just...I came up with it a couple of days ago and I thought it was good. It's what you have to do.

"One of the problems that a lot of people like myself — we have very high levels of intelligence, but we're not necessarily such believers."

"I don't have temper tantrums. I really don't."

"My ratings are the highest since the World Trade Center came down."

"We have accomplished more than any president in the first year, by far."

"I have many, many-just so you understand, I have many attorneys. I have attorneys-sadly, I have so many attorneys you wouldn't even believe it."

"He speaks and his people sit up at attention. I want my people to do the same." (About Kim Jong-un)

"I would give myself an A+"

To a rally in Minnesota:
"Hispanic American unemployment has reached its lowest level ever recorded the history our country. And remember, I'd go into big stadiums like this that were packed?"

"And by the way, you're very good at real estate. Did you see the thousands and thousands of people outside?"

"And I usually go home my wife would say "How was the crowd?" Although honestly, when you have many thousands of people like have tonight- you know, I was at an event three weeks ago where a person from the New York Times said, "There was only a thousand people.""
"And we all have ego, but I don't want to show my face. I want to show the crowds. It's much prettier. Because you people are incredible. Unemployment among women has reach the lowest level as of today in 65 years."

"But I'll tell you, to keep this incredible momentum, I think maybe the most successful that the country has ever had. And you know, I went to people- I thought about it- I thought, oh, I think I'm such a genius."

"So we've made this incredible progress together with your help, with the help of the millions and millions of people that- well, some polls got it right. But not all polls got it right."

"Why are they elite? I have a much better apartment than they do. I'm smarter than they are. I'm richer than they are. I became president* and they didn't."

At CPAC 2018 speech pointing to a picture of himself: "What a nice picture that is. Look at that- I'd love to watch that guy speak. Oh boy. That's nice. I try like hell to hide that bald spot folks, I work hard at it. Doesn't look bad— we're hanging in- we're hanging in. We're hanging in there- together we're hanging in."

"I don't know how you can impeach somebody who's done a great job."

Right after the riot and protests in Charlottesville VA:
"I own a house in Charlottesville, Does anyone know I own a house in Charlottesville?
Oh boy, it's gonna be... it's in Charlottesville. It is the winery. I mean, I know a lot about Charlottesville. Charlottesville is a great place that's been very badly hurt of the last couple of day. I own actually one of the largest wineries in the United State, it's in Charlottesville."

"Hey! I'm the President* of the United States! I'm not the president* of the globe."

"I want to give a victory speech."

"Every time a person comes in to the Oval Office, a president, a king, a queen, a prime minister they say, Mr. President*, congratulations on what you've done with this country. It's true."

October 17, 2018
"What are you going to do in 6 1/2 years with a normal boring person here?"

"Look, I'm 48 and 1 in the primaries, and actually it's much higher than that because I endorsed a lot of people that were successful that people don't even talk about."

"And I was getting literally tens of thousands of people, also, more than Hillary in the same location!"

"We have a witch hunt now going on, and I handle it very well, and there was no collusion. Everyone knows it. It's —- people laugh."

"I would say , without question, first two years of office, I've had the most successful two year in the history of this country as a president."

"I have the most successful. Nobody has done what I've done, and nobody has come close in the first two years of office. here, these are just some. I just put them down rough. But take a look at that- you all set.
Who is the one, who's the one president that percentage-wise has done better than me? There's only one. George Washington - 100%. Nobody has gotten that yet."

"I'm just saying, I just speak for myself. You take a look, and you make your own determination."

"Nobody has been better at the military."

"Because I have created such an incredible economy, I have created so many jobs. I have made this country with you so great that everybody wants to come in."

"Obstruction. You know, I just walked in, and a big, strong guy grabbed me. And he was almost crying. It happens every time. And many times. And he said, 'sir, Mr. President,, thank you so much for saving our country'."

About being in disaster areas in his hair:
"And you walk around in those conditions, you can't fake it. You can't fake it. So that's one good thing. Nobody every says that any more. That's one of the- might be one of the best things that's happened to me in a long time."

"Barbara Walters interviewed me. Do you mind if I play with your hair? Do you remember that? And then numerous people have don that. But that's ok. But the choice could not be more clear. Democrats produce mobs. Republicans produce jobs."

About Joe Biden:
"Remember, he challenged me to a fight, and that was fine. And when I said he wouldn't last long, he'd be down faster than Greg would take him down. He'd be down so fast. Remember? Faster than Greg. I'd have to go very fast. I'd have to immediately connect."

Feb 16, 2017
Press conference
"I'm here today to update the American people on the incredible progress that has been made in the last four weeks since my inauguration. We have made incredible progress. I don't think there's ever been a President elected who, in this short period of time, has done what we've done.
I turn on the TV, open the newspapers, and I see stories of chaos. Chaos! Yet, it is the exact opposite. This administration is running like a fine-tuned machine, despite the fact that I can't get my Cabinet approved, and they're outstanding people. Like Senator Dan Coates whose there -- one of the most respected men of the Senate -- he can't get approved. How do you not approve him? He's been a colleague, highly

respected -- brilliant guy, great guy, everybody knows it -- but waiting for approval.

And the wall is going to be a great wall, and it's going to be a wall negotiated by me. The price is going to come down, just like it has on everything else I've negotiated for the government. And we're going to have a wall that works. We're not going to have a wall like they have now, which is either nonexistent or a joke."

"This last month has represented an unprecedented degree of action on behalf of the great citizens of our country. Again, I say it -- there has never been a presidency that's done so much in such a short period of time. And we haven't even started the big work that starts early next week. Some very big things are going to be announced next week."

At the UN:
"In less than two years, my administration has accomplished more than almost any administration in the history of our country. America's— (laughter in the audience)— so true— Didn't expect that reaction, but that's okay."

About Angelina Jolie:
"I really understand beauty. And I will tell you, she's not - I do own Miss Universe. I do own Miss USA. I mean I own a lot of different things. I do understand beauty, and she's not."

"All of the women on The Apprentice flirted with me - consciously or unconsciously. That's to be expected."

"Anyone who thinks my story is anywhere near over is sadly mistaken."

"I wouldn't mind a little bow. In Japan, they bow. I love it. Only thing I love about Japan."

"I had great relationship with the Hispanic - we had a lot of Hispanics in the school actually from different countries, Venezuela, from Brazil, and they all played soccer, and I was on the soccer team, and I developed great relationships with them."

"Jimmy Carter used to walk off the airplane carrying his own luggage. Do you remember that? I don't want my president carrying - I want the freaking Marines to be carrying his luggage, and they want to carry his luggage."

"Somebody made the statement that Donald Trump has built or owns the greatest collection of golf courses, ever, in the history of golf. And I believe that is 100 percent true."

10-15-17
"There are those that are saying it's one of the finest group of people ever assembled as a candidate — as a Cabinet. This is a tremendous amount of talent. We have just gotten really, really, great people. I'm very proud of them.

10-13-17 at Value Voters Summit:

"When I came to speak with you last year, I made you a promise. Well, one of the promises I made you was that I'd come back. See? And I don't even need your vote this year, right? That's even nicer."

About an address to Congress:
"A lot of the people have said that, some people said it was the single best speech ever made in that chamber."

"I have a real passion for learning. My books and my professional experience always included a strong education or "lessons learned" slant. This book is a collection of my beliefs and about business and life-my basic rules and principles. It also contains questions submitted to me on the Trump University blog and my answers."

"You know, people don't understand. I went to an Ivy League college- I was a nice student-I did very well-I'm a very intelligent person-"

"Look, I accomplished the military. I accomplished the tax cuts. I accomplished the regulation cuts. I accomplished so much. The economy is the number one economy in the whole world. We're the number one- not even close. Companies are pouring into our country. I've accomplished so much."

"I had a senator in my office, he said, 'You know, Mr. President*, I've run six times and I'll tell you, out of six times and I've won four.' And I was just kidding, I said, well, you know what -- and he was a senator and he was a congressman -- I said, 'I won -- I ran one time for the president of the

United States and out of one time I won one. I'm one for one.' And he sort of laughed and it's never happened before, nobody's ever done that."

"So Prime Minister Abe gave- it's the most beautiful 5 letter- 5 page letter- Nobel Prize- he sent it to them- you know why? He had rocket ships and missiles flying over Japan, and they had alarms going off- you know that. Now all of a sudden they feel good. They feel safe. I did that. And it was a very tough dialog at the beginning. Fire and fury- total anhilation- my button is bigger than yours and my button works- you remember that? You don't remember that. And people said- Trump is crazy. And you know what it ended up being? A very good relationship. I like Kim a lot and he likes me a lot. Nobody else would have done that. The Obama administration couldn't have done that. Number one they probably wouldn't have done it and number two they didn't have the capability to do it."

"They can do presidential harassment, put very simply, and I'll be very good at handling that and I think I'll be better than anybody in the history of this office."

"There's never been an impact- I don't say it braggingly. I mean, it's hard for me to say it because I'd rather have them say it but they don't say it very well. No, there's never been a story, nobody ever writes it. Pretty impressive if I do say so myself."

About being thankful:
"For having a great family. And for having made a tremendous difference in this country. I've made a tremendous difference in the country. This country is so much

113

stronger now than it was when I took office you wouldn't believe it. I mean you see it- but so much stronger than people can't even believe it. When I see foreign leaders they say "We cannot believe the difference in strength between the United States now and the United States two years ago. Made a lot of progress."

11-27-18
"Tupelo, home of thousands of hard-working American patriots, and the proud birthplace of the king of rock n roll, Elvis. Elvis! We love Elvis!
I shouldn't say this, you'll say I'm very conceited, because I'm not, but other than the blonde hair, when I was growing up they said I looked like Elvis. Can you believe it? I always considered that a great compliment. We love Elvis, don't we?"

"Wow, this is great. Look snow! I didn't know what was going on. This is - I said, you sure this is indoor? That beautiful snow looks so real.
That's the end of my suit. That's the end of the hair for tonight.
You know, we had a fantastic evening and day very recently, the midterms. We got very little credit from the fake news media.
They talked about the House, but the people I campaigned for in the House, which was very few, I can't - look, I'm one person."

"Now they call me a politician. I'm a politician. I can't stand it. They said he's a political person. But I've only had one race, and look at the result. You know that. You know that. You know that. You know what I'm talking about."

"I have absolute right to do what I want to do with the Justice Department."

"Nobody's done more for the military than I have. I took the budget from very little to $700 billion- $716 billion and I'm now going over to the Coast Guard where I did last year and will probably a lot. But we're going over to the Coast Guard and I just really believe nobody in fact a number of generals were on television over the weekend, unrelated, but they all mentioned that nobody's done as a president for the military in a long time what I've done."

"I happen to be a tariff person because I'm a smart person, OK?"

"One of the problems that a lot of people like myself, we have very high levels of intelligence but we're not necessarily such believers…"

At a rally 3/28/19
"We're the elite. You are smarter. You are and sharper. Your more loyal. You're a hell of lot tougher."

"I have a better education than them, I'm smarter than them, I went to the best schools, they didn't. Much more beautiful house, much more beautiful apartment. Much more beautiful everything. And I'm president* and they're not."

"I get a kick I hear, so and so, the elite and then you see this guy like this little schlepper. This is elite? I'm not elite. This is elite? We're the elite. You're smarter. You're sharper. You're more loyal. You're a hell of a lot tougher, a hell of a lot tougher.

Thank you Donald."

"We did great with women and I think we're going to do better with women now."

"I will never, ever stop and we are winning so big. Nobody thought it could happen."

"Iran is a MUCH DIFFERENT COUNTRY than it was when I became president*."

"I think I would have been a good general, but who knows?"

About Syria:

"It's not my fault. I didn't put us there. Syria was lost long ago..We are talking about sand and death. We are not taking about vast wealth."

"I know more about drones than anybody."

"I've kept more promises than I made."

"But, you know, I never did politics before. Now I do politics. In the meantime, I built a lot of wall. I have a lot of money, and I built a lot of wall."

"I can tell you I have the support of the police, the support of the military, the support of the bikers for Trump- I have the tough people, but they don't play it tough- until they go to a certain point, and then it would be bad, very bad."

"And I see suffering. I mean, I see tremendous suffering and I understand. I have a very big heart. A lot of people don't understand that, but people that know me do. And we have to take care of our country, and I do feel America first. I mean, America has been fourth and fifth and ninth. I mean…"

August 21, 2019:

"I am the chosen one."

"I look very much forward to showing my financials, because they are huge."

The Investigation

(Denial. Total denial. Or, total involvement.)

"I didn't know anything about it. Nothing about it." (about Paul Manafort sharing polling info with Russians)

"The other thing is -- this (Michael Cohen legal situation) wasn't me. This was having to do with the taxi industry or something. But he has -- and financing, but nothing to do with me."

"I could sit down with Democrats and work this thing out in one hour. And we need a wall. We have to have a wall. We're building a wall now, but we should build it very fast. We should build it -- frankly, we should build it even higher, because these people -- incredible. They can scale them; they can do things you wouldn't believe. But we have a wall, it's going up."

"Do you think she leaked? She leaked. She leaked. Remember that? No, I didn't leak, remember? Remember? Senator John Cornyn, great guy from Texas. He asked a question. 'Did you leak?' She was startled, because she was unprepared. 'No -- no -- did -- what? Did I leak? No, no, we didn't leak, no. No, we didn't leak.' That was the worst body language I think I've ever seen. Remember? Remember Jon Lovitz, the liar, remember Jon Lovitz? 'Yeah, yeah, I'm a businessman, that's right. I went to -- yeah, yeah, I went to Harvard. Yeah, that's right. I went to Harvard. I'm a businessman.' That was, like, a female version of Jon Lovitz."

"It's nothing more than a witch hunt. And most people get it, including Democrats. They wink at me. They look at me, they wink at me. The Democrats get it too."

"Totally clears the President. Thank you!"

"It turned out with Russia there was collusion, but it was with Hillary Clinton, the DNC."

On who's been the toughest on Russia:
"You can ask President Putin about that. There's been nobody. So there's no collusion whatsoever."

"I've take the position- and I don't have to take this position and maybe I'll change- that I will not be involved with the Justice Department. I will wait until this is over."

"A horrible thing and yet, I've accomplished, with all of this going on, more than any president in the first year in our history. Even the enemies and the haters admit that."

"We have accomplished more than any president in the first year, by far."

"I have many, many-just so you understand, I have many attorneys. I have attorneys-sadly, I have so many attorneys you wouldn't even believe it."

"Michael Cohen represents me- like with this crazy Stormy Daniels deal he represented me. But I'm not involved and I'm not involved - and I've been told I'm not involved."

"There is no collusion with me."

About talking to Mueller:
"They're getting people who say something that is a little bit off. "Is it a nice day?" "Well, you know, no it's not a great day." Oops— he lied. People are afraid of that. I would like to talk but it seems to be very biased."

"The problem with the Mueller investigation is everybody's got massive conflicts. You have this person who was at Hillary Clinton's funeral. Meaning her party that turned into a funeral. They were screaming, crying, going crazy. I call them the 13 angry Democrats. You have tremendous animosity."

"They put the two counts of campaign violations in there, but a lot of lawyers on television, and also lawyers that I have say- they're not even crimes."

"Obstruction. You know, I just walked in, and a big, strong guy grabbed me. And he was almost crying. It happens every time. And many times. And he said, 'sir, Mr. President,, thank you so much for saving our country'."

"If I ever called the Russians, the first one to know about it would be the state of Montana, and they wouldn't be too happy. Can you imagine? Let's call the Russians? It's a disgrace."

Q: Did you fire Mike Flynn?
Mike Flynn is a fine person, and I asked for his resignation. He respectfully gave it. He is a man who -- there was a certain amount of information given to Vice President Pence, who is with us today. And I was not happy with the way that information was given.He didn't have to do that, because what he did wasn't wrong, what he did in terms of the information he saw. What was wrong was the way that other people, including yourselves in this room, were given that information, because that was classified information that was given illegally. That's the real problem.

"That's not the FBI. That's a fix."

About Putin
"He doesn't respect our president. And if it is Russia -- which it's probably not, nobody knows who it is - but it if is Russia, it's really bad for a different reason. Because it shows how little respect they have for our country when they would hack into a major party and get everything. But it would be interesting to see -- I will tell you this: Russia, if you're listening, I hope you're able to find the 30,000 emails that are missing. I think you will probably be rewarded mightily by our press. Let's see if that happens. That'll be next."

"Oh' I see! Now that the 2 year Russian Collusion case has fallen apart, there was no Collusion except by Crooked Hillary and the Democrats, they say, 'gee, I have an idea, let's look at Trump's finances and every deal he has ever done."

"The only Collusion with the Russians was with Crooked Hillary Clinton and the Democratic National Committee."

Tweeting 12/10/18
Democrats can't find a Smocking Gun tying the Trump campaign to Russia after James Comey's testimony. No Smocking Gun… No Collusion.

The famous Lester Holt interview in May 2017
"He [Rosenstein] made a recommendation, he's highly respected, very good guy, very smart guy. The Democrats like him, the Republicans like him. He made a recommendation. But regardless of [the] recommendation, I was going to fire Comey. Knowing there was no good time to do it! And in fact when I decided to just do it I said to myself, I said, 'You know, this Russia thing with Trump and Russia is a made-up story, it's an excuse by the Democrats for having lost an election that they should've won'."

4/2/19
"I hope they now go and take a look at the oranges, the oranges of the investigation, the beginnings of that investigation. You look at the origin of the investigation, where it started, how it started, who started it, whether it's McCabe or Comey or a lot of them. Where does it go, how high up in the White House did it go? You will all get Pulitzer

Prizes, ok? You'll all get Pulitzer Prizes. You should have looked at it a long time ago and that's the only thing that's disappointing to me about the Mueller report.
"The Mueller report I wished covered the oranges, how it started, the beginnings of the investigation, how it started. It didn't cover that, and for some reason none of that was discussed."

"So there's no collusion whatsoever."

"My son's a good young guy."

"And even people that are not my friends say that was a horrible thing that he did to the president*, a horrible thing."

"I could fire him whenever I want to fire him, but I haven't said that I was going to. I just haven't said I was going to fire him. We'll see what happens. But if you ask me: am I thrilled? No, I am not thrilled." (about Jeff Sessions)

In Fear: Trump in the White House:
"They're out to get me. This is an injustice. This is unfair. How could this have happened? It's all Jeff Sessions' fault. This is all politically motivated. Rod Rosenstein doesn't know the the hell he is doing. He's a Democrat. He's from Maryland."

"Oh my God. This is terrible. This is the end of my Presidency. I'm fucked. How could you let this happen, Jeff?"

"Everyone tells me if you get one of these independent counsels it ruins your presidency. It takes years and years and

I won't be able to do anything. This is the worst thing that ever happened to me."

"So they're investigating something that never happened."

"No collusion. No collusion."

The Wall

(That elusive, yet ever present Wall. Magnificent!)

"We will have the greatest borders, the greatest walls."

"When that wall went up, it's a whole different ball game. ... I don't care whether a mayor is a Republican or a Democrat. They're full of crap when they say it hasn't made a big difference. I heard the same thing from the fake news. They said, 'Oh crime, it actually stayed the same.' It didn't stay the same. It went way down. ... Thanks to a powerful border wall in El Paso, Texas, it's one of America's safest cities now."

"And the wall is going to be a great wall, and it's going to be a wall negotiated by me. The price is going to come down, just like it has on everything else I've negotiated for the government. And we're going to have a wall that works. We're not going to have a wall like they have now, which is either nonexistent or a joke."

"An all concrete Wall was NEVER ABANDONED, as has been reported by the media. Some areas will be all concrete but the experts at Border Patrol prefer a Wall that is see through (thereby making it possible to see what is happening on both sides). Makes sense to me!

"It's like the wheel, there is nothing better, I know tech better than anyone & technology on a Border is only effective in conjunction with a Wall."

At a press conference:

"Here we go again. (question about the wall and his promise to a female reporter)

A very nice question and beautifully asked.

Excuse me- excuse me. Are you ready? you ready? I just told you we just made a trade deal. We will take in billions and billions of dollars. Far more than the cost of the wall. The wall is peanuts compared to what the value of this trade deal is to the United States. As far as concrete- I said I was going to build a wall- I never said "I'm gonna build a concrete"- Just so you don't- cuz I now you're not into the construction business. You don't understand something- we now have a great steel business that's rebuilt in the United States. STEEL is stronger than concrete. If I build this wall or this fence or anything the Democrats want to call it- I'm not into names- I'm into production. I'm into something that works. If I build a steel wall rather than a concrete wall it will actually be stronger than a concrete- steel is stronger that concrete, okay? You can check it out. Listen- if I build a wall, and the wall is made out of steel instead of concrete I think people will like that. And here's the other good thing- I'll have it done by the United States steel corporations. I'll have it done by companies that are now in our country that are powerful."

"When during the campaign, I would say 'Mexico is going to pay for it,' obviously, I never said this, and I never meant they're gonna write out a check, I said they're going to pay for it. They are."

1-30-19
"We are building a lot of wall- you know— I'm not waiting for this committee."

"Ninety per cent of the drugs don't come through the port of entry. Ninety per cent of the drugs and the big stuff goes out to the desert, makes a left, and goes where you don't have any wall."

"So, finally, to protect our communities, we must secure the border against human trafficking, drug smuggling, and crime of all types. The human trafficking is a tremendous problem where, mostly women, and they're tied up and they're taped up, and they're put in the back of cars, and the car does not come through the port of entry."

"We're doing very well on the wall. We're building a lot of wall right now."

"In fact, I hear the Democrats want to take down all walls along the southern border."

Announcing national emergency
"I want to thank Mexico. They have their own problems. They have the largest number of murders that they've ever

had in their history -- almost 40,000 murders. Forty thousand."

"You can't take human traffic -- women and girls -- you can't take them through ports of entry. You can't have them tied up in the backseat of a car or a truck or a van. They open the door. They look. They can't see three women with tape on their mouth or three women whose hands are tied. They go through areas where you have no wall. Everybody knows that. Nancy knows it. Chuck knows it. They all know it. It's all a big lie. It's a big con game."

"Human trafficking by airplane is almost impossible. Human trafficking by van and truck, in the backseat of a car, and going through a border where there's nobody for miles and miles, and there's no wall to protect -- it's very easy."

"And unlike what the Democrats say, they don't, you don't bring trucks of drugs through the checkpoints. You bring trucks of drugs by making a right 20 miles, and a left into the country. They're not bringing, you know, they bring massive amounts of drugs, and they do it because there's no barrier, there's no hardened wall that you can't knock down with your breath."

"Open borders are very bad for our country. Crime comes in. Drugs, human trafficking, so many things. But let's talk about human trafficking. You can't bring women or children through a port of entry, where you have people looking into the back of a car or a van, a truck. It has to go out into the open areas, where they drive into our country like there's no problem, and that's exactly what they do. They get off the main drag, or the main road. They make a right, or a left, and then they come right into our country. They go through areas where there is nobody."

Speaking about ending the government shutdown
"Human traffickers -- the victims are women and children. Maybe to a lesser extent, believe or not, children. Women are tied up. They're bound. Duct tape put around their faces, around their mouths. In many cases, they can't even breathe. They're put in the backs of cars or vans or trucks. they don't go through your port of entry. They make a right turn going very quickly. They go into the desert areas, or whatever areas you can look at. And as soon as there's no protection, they make a left or a right into the United States of America. There's nobody to catch them. There's nobody to find them. They can't come through the port, because if they come through the port, people will see four women sitting in a van with tape around their face and around their mouth. Can't have that. And that problem, because of the Internet, is the biggest problem -- it's never been like this before -- that you can imagine. It's at the worst level -- human trafficking -- in the history of the world. This is not a United States problem; this is a world problem. But they come through areas where they have no protection, where they have no steel barriers, where they have no walls. And we can stop almost 100 per cent of that."

February 25, 2019 speaking to governors:
"These people, they have, they have the traffickers, they're vicious, they're smart- the coyotes. How 'bout the name- the coyotes? They have people tied up- put up in the back of

trucks and vans. They can't go through checkpoints- they have to go through…open areas. You can't walk through-you can't go through cuz even if they don't do much of an inspection of your truck or your car, they do open the back door or look through a window - you can't have women sitting there that are tied up. So when I hear the other side say, and we have some from the other side here, but when I hear the other side say "oh no, everything goes through the checkpoints" - that's absolutely false. You have areas where you literally have roads that are carved in the sand and are used so much. They go right through these roads, they go right, they hang a left, hang another left and welcome to the United States there's nobody there to even talk to them. Cuz you're talking about two thousand miles! You're talking about a lot of area. So we're doing really well…"

"And by the way- the USMCA, from Mexico - that's United States Mexico and Canada- that's where the money's coming from, not directly but indirectly, for the wall. And nobody wants to talk about that. Because we're saving billions and billions of dollars a year- if Congress approves that deal. Now they might not want to approve a deal just because they'll say— one of the things I'm thinking of doing- this has never been done before-no matter how good a deal I make with China - if they sell me Beijing for $1 dollar, if they give me 50% of their land and every ship that they've built over the last two years, which is a lot -and they give them to me free - the Democrats will say- what a lousy deal - that's a terrible deal."

At Mar-a-Lago 11/24/18

"The 9th Circuit, everybody knows it's totally out of control. What they're doing, what they're saying, the opinions are very unfair to law enforcement, they're very unfair to our military, and they're very unfair most importantly to the people of our country, cuz I'm keeping them safe. And you've seen how we've fortified things, and all of that, all of that vast amount of fighting you see going on at the border, it's all taking place in Mexico. And Mexico cannot believe how tough these people are. The mayor of Tijuana and many others have said, "Boy, these are tough people." They start fighting right away. They're tough people. Many criminals in that caravan.

"There are tremendously dangerous people in those caravans. We do not want them coming in to the United States and we're not gonna let em. We're throwing them out- MS13 and so many others. We're throwing them out of our country by the thousands that got in here over the years. We're throwing them out by the thousands and we're bringing back towns and we're making them safe and we're doing an excellent job. Even our legislation that we passed- it failed in the 9th Circuit, it failed in the 9th Circuit appeal then it won in the Supreme Court. And it's just a shame because it's really hurting people. It's hurting our law enforcement tremendously, and now that the military's on the border it's really hurting our military. And frankly when they hear these decisions these are professionals the military the law enforcement the first responders- they can't believe the decisions that are being made by these judges. This is what they do , they do law enforcement law and order and they get these decisions and they say who makes these decisions? They're not into lawyer things."

Question about troops at the border.

"No -no troops. We're going to have a strong border. Our southern border is going to be very strong... you gotta have borders. You don't have borders you don't have a country."

What about the military using lethal force?
"They're going to have to use lethal force- I've given the okay.
Bad things are happening in Tijuana. But not in this country, because I closed it up I actually two days ago we closed the border. We actually just closed it. We said nobody's coming in because it was so out of control.
"And Mexico will not be able to sell their cars into the United States where they make so many cars at great benefit to them, not at great benefit to us.
I've already shut it down (the border) - I've already shut it down- for short periods. I've already shut down parts of the border because it was out of control with the rioting on the other side in Mexico. I just said shut it down. You see it. It took place two days ago. Yeah- they call me up and I sign an order.
"Can we get a copy of that?"
"Aaah— you don't need that. Don't worry- it's not that big a deal. But maybe to some people it is."

Tweet 12/21/18
The Democrats are trying to belittle the concept of a Wall, calling it old fashioned. The fact is there is nothing else's that will work, and that hass been true for thousands of years. It's like the wheel, there is nothing better. I know tech better than anyone, & technology on a Border is only effective in conjunction with a Wall.

When signing the 2018 Farm bill

"A nation without borders is not a nation at all. Without borders, we have the reign of chaos, crime, and - believe it or not- coyotes."

"The wheel, the wall, some things never get old."

"Before I close the border, Mexico—we love Mexico, we love the country of Mexico—we have two problems: We have the fact that they allow people to pour into our country. We have to stop 'em. Border Patrol has been incredible. ICE has been incredible. Law enforcement has been incredible. And the other problem is drugs. Massive amounts of...a large...most of the drugs, much of the drugs coming into our country come through the southern border. In all different ways. Much of it where we don't have walls—the wall is under construction by the way. Large sections. We're going to be meeting, I think on Friday, at a piece of the wall that we've completed. A big piece. A lot of it's being built right now. Lot of its being signed up right now by different contractors. It's moving along very nicely. But we need the wall. But we need lots of other things. So we need help from Mexico. If Mexico doesn't give the help, that's okay. We're gonna tariff their cars coming into the United States.
"The other thing is because Mexico is such a big source of drugs—unfortunately, unfortunately. Now we have China sending fentanyl to Mexico so it can be delivered into the United States. It's not acceptable. So, the second aspect of it is, which you haven't heard before, is that if the drugs don't stop—Mexico can stop 'em if they want—we're gonna tariff the cars. The cars are very big. And if that doesn't work, we're gonna close the border."

"Mexico is paying for the Wall through the new USMCA Trade Deal."

"China and by the way we are building that wall as you -- we are building that wall. Build it. It's faster and it's less expensive and it's also much more beautiful.
They do anything they can -- you're a shifty shift."

Healthcare?

(We all should be so confident that he will get this fixed too!)

"Democrats' plan to destroy health care also includes raiding Medicare to fund benefits for illegal immigrants. Not something that Indiana is really thrilled about. "

"And Republicans will always protect patients with pre-existing conditions."

"Because Obamacare is too expensive, the premiums are way too high, and the deductibles don't exist. I mean, the deductibles, you can't even use it. The deductible is so high. Unless you get hit by a tractor, you can't even use it. Nobody has ever seen anything like it. The deductibles are so high."

"We were going in for a routine repeal and replace, and he went thumbs down. Not nice. That was not nice."

"As far as single payer, it works in Canada. It works incredibly well in Scotland."

"Obamacare is, number one and maybe least importantly, it's costing the country a fortune."

"Once you get something for pre-existing conditions, etc., etc. Once you get something, it's awfully tough to take it away. As they get something, it gets tougher. Because politically, you can't give it away. So pre-existing conditions are a tough deal."

"And Republicans will always protect Americans with pre-existing conditions.
So, the wall has started, very, very substantially."

"We have to come up, and we can come up with many different plans. In fact, plans you don't even know about will be devised because we're going to come up with plans-healthcare plans- that will be so good."

"We will not rest until Americans have the healthcare system that they need and deserve: a system that finally puts American patients first. We say 'America first. America patients first.'   "You've worked so hard on these things, you've worked so hard on the kidney, very special, the kidney has a very special place in the heart, it's an incredible thing. People that have to go this … people have loved ones that are working so hard to stay alive, they have to work so hard. There's an esprit de corps spirit, like you see rarely on anything, so I just want to thank all you folks for being here, it's really fantastic, and it's truly an exciting day for advancing kidney health in our country."

"And we will also protect you with pre-existing physicians. How about that? Pre-existing physicians. The first time I've ever said that. Just thought of that! It's true because under their plans, you don't get your own doctor. You know what you get? Whatever the hell you get. That's what you get. Oh great doc, fix me up doc. You mean you want to work on my heart? Who are you, doc? I don't think so."

Sensitivity, Consideration and Courtesy

(Such a great example of civility and class.)

"Oh, we have a single protester. There we go. Goodbye, darling. Goodbye, darling.
Was that a man or a woman? Because he needs a haircut more than I do. It's true. I couldn't tell. Needs a haircut."

After the hurricane Trump was talking to a man whose house was damaged by a large boat shipwrecked in his yard
"Is this your boat?"
The man said no.
"At least you got a nice boat out of the deal."

And handing out meals to victims
"Have a good time.."

"Hispanic, any Hispanic here? I think so. Any Asians? Asian? Asian? Any Asian?"

About Angelina Jolie
"I really understand beauty. And I will tell you, she's not - I do own Miss Universe. I do own Miss USA. I mean I own a lot of different things. I do understand beauty, and she's not."

Respect for Women:

About Hillary- making mocking movements
"But here's a woman- she's supposed to fight all these different things, and she can't make it fifteen feet to her car- give me a break. Give me a break. GIVE ME A BREAK! She's home resting right now- she's getting ready for her next speech. It's going to be about fifteen minutes"

To Brigette Trogneux, wife of French President Macron gesturing toward her body: "You know, you're in such good shape." And then to her husband: "Beautiful"

About Katarina Witt, Olympian:
"Wonderful looking while on the ice but up close and personal, she could only be described as attractive if you like a woman with a bad complexion who is built like a linebacker".

To Howard Stern about having bought the Miss USA pageant

"They said, 'How are you going to change the pageant?' I said 'I'm going to get the bathing suits to be smaller and the heels to be higher'. If you're looking for a rocket scientist, don't tune in tonight, but if you're looking for a really beautiful woman, you should watch."

Humility:

"All of the women on The Apprentice flirted with me - consciously or unconsciously. That's to be expected."

About Carly Fiorina- candidate for president
"Look at that face. Would anyone vote for that? Can you imagine that, the face of our next next President? I mean, she's a woman, and I'm not supposed to say bad things, but really, folks, come on. Are we serious?"

8/28/12:
"@ariannahuff is unattractive both inside and out. I fully understand why her former husband left her for a man- he made a good decision."

"Why are we having all these people from shithole countries coming here?"

The Shut-Down

(This was a fine example of diplomacy at work...)

"I tell you what, I am proud to shut down the government for border security, Chuck, because the people of this country don't want criminals and people that have lots of problems and drugs pouring into our country. So, I will take the mantle. I will be the one to shut it down. I'm not going to blame you for it. The last time you shut it down it didn't work. I will take the mantle of shutting down and I'm going to shut it down for border security."

About what Wilbur Ross said to government workers getting loans
"No, I haven't -- I haven't heard the statement, but I do understand that perhaps he should have said it differently. Local people know who they are when they go for groceries and everything else. And I think what Wilbur was probably trying to say is that they will work along. I know banks are working along. If you have mortgages, the mortgagees -- the mortgage -- the folks collecting the interest and all of those

things, they work along. And that's what happens in times like this. They know the people. They've been dealing with them for years. And they work along. The grocery store -- and I think that's probably what Wilbur Ross meant, but I haven't seen his statement, no."

"I'm looking at things and I've got a lot of options."

Tweet January 15, 2019
The Clemson football team at the WH during the shutdown McDonald's, Wendy's and Burger King's with some pizza. I think that would be their favorite food, so we'll see what happens.
Because of the shutdown, you know we have the great Clemson team with us, the national champions. So we went out and we ordered American fast food, paid for by me. Lots of hamburgers, lot of pizza.
We have some very large people that like eating. So I think we're going to have a little fun. If it's American, I like it. It's all American stuff- 300 hamburgers, many, many French fries —all of our favorite foods.

"I very calmly said, 'If you're not going to give us strong borders, bye-bye.' And I left. I didn't rant. I didn't rave, like you reported."

"I don't have temper tantrums. I really don't."

"I didn't smash the table. I should have, but I didn't smash the table."

"A shut-down falls on the President's lack of leadership. He can't even control his party and get people in the same room. A shut-down means the President is weak."   From 2013.

The Best Words

(They speak for themselves…)

And from a clip that was created by the Daily Show. The spelling of The Best Words is accurate to how they were pronounced.

"From the Wright Brothers to that beautiful Orion space cap-sickle…"

"To ensure the endurance of our nation as a sahven country…"

"The wall is under construction, a lot of work has been done, a lot of renoversh if you look at some of it…"

"And he voted for ObamNa amnesty…"

"By a sleazebag lawyer named Avianti…"

"Joining us from Al Jabbar air base in Kuwait is the central command Chris response and crisis response…"

"We don't want you to put defensive mishus and missiles…"

"Special Agent Celestino Martinez, he goes by DJ, and CJ, he said call me other one…"

"And significantly beating expectations in the House for the midtowm and midturn year…"

"The op-ed published in the failing New York Times by anonomess really anomis…"

"Who were kidnapped by Boca Harram in April of 20,014…"

"Merry chrissus erry everybody! We just have to say it all together."

"The word is 'sow', and old English term."

Montana rally 9-7-18. (spelling is as close to his pronunciation as we can get)
"The latest act of resistance is the op-ed published in the failing New York Times by an anonmous, really an inomis, gutless coward."

10-2-19
"Believe it or not, I watch my words very carefully. There are those that think I'm a very stable genius, okay? I watch my words very, very closely. And to have somebody get up, and to totally fabricate a conversation that I had with another leader, and make it sound so bad. It was so evil."

"Despite the constant negative press covfefe."

I Have No Idea

(What if he was in your living room? I think it would be
something like this...)

"Now, the arena holds 8,000, and thank you fire department,
they got in about 10. Thank you fire department, appreciate
it."

"Look, having nuclear — my uncle was a great professor and
scientist and engineer, Dr. John Trump at MIT; good genes,
very good genes, OK, very smart, the Wharton School of
Finance, very good, very smart — you know, if you're a
conservative Republican, if I were a liberal, if, like, OK, if I
ran as a liberal Democrat, they would say I'm one of the
smartest people anywhere in the world — it's true! — but
when you're a conservative Republican they try — oh, do
they do a number — that's why I always start off: Went to
Wharton, was a good student, went there, went there, did this,
built a fortune — you know I have to give my like credentials
all the time, because we're a little disadvantaged — but you
look at the nuclear deal, the thing that really bothers me — it
would have been so easy, and it's not as important as these

146

lives are — nuclear is powerful; my uncle explained that to me many, many years ago, the power and that was 35 years ago; he would explain the power of what's going to happen and he was right, who would have thought? — but when you look at what's going on with the four prisoners — now it used to be three, now it's four — but when it was three and even now, I would have said it's all in the messenger; fellas, and it is fellas because, you know, they don't, they haven't figured that the women are smarter right now than the men, so, you know, it's gonna take them about another 150 years — but the Persians are great negotiators, the Iranians are great negotiators, so, and they, they just killed, they just killed us."

And here's Donald Trump's speech. After Charlottesville, delivered in Phoenix.

TRUMP: But all the networks — I mean, CNN is really bad, but ABC this morning — I don't watch it much, but I'm watching in the morning, and they have little George Stephanopoulos talking to Nikki Haley, right? Little George.

And — and he talks about the speech I made last night, which believe it or not, got great reviews, right?

They had a hard time. They were having a hard time because it was with soldiers, we were somber, we were truthful, we were doing — we were saying things — and it really did.

So, he talked about it for like that much, then he goes, "Let's get back to Charlottesville." Charlottesville. And Nikki was great. She's doing a great job, by the way.

So now, I say we have to heal our wounds and the wounds of our country. I love the people of our country, the people, all of the people. It says I love all of the people of our country.

I didn't say I love you because you're black, or I love you because you're white, or I love you because you're from Japan, or you're from China, or you're from Kenya, or you're from Scotland or Sweden. I love all the people of our country.

So, I said here's my — this is — by the way folks, this is my exact words: "I love all the people of our country. We're going to make America great again, but we're going to make it great for all of the people of the United States of America."

And then they say, is he a racist? Is he a racist? Then, I did a second one. So then I did a second one.

Don't bother, it's only a single voice. And not a very powerful voice.

How did he get in here? He's supposed to be with the few people outside.

How about — how about all week they're talking about the massive crowds that are going to be outside. Where are they? Well, it's hot out. It is hot. I think it's too warm.

You know, they show up in the helmets and the black masks, and they've got clubs and they've got everything — Antifa!

So on August the 14th — so that was it, and I said all people, I love all people, everything, right? Now I figure I'm going to do it again. I'll be even more specific.

So I said, based on the events that took place over the last weekend in Charlottesville, I'd like to provide the nation with an update. Because that was right after the event, the first one, right?

An update on ongoing federal response to the horrific attack and violence that was witnessed by everybody. To anyone who acted criminally in this weekend's racist violence, you will be held fully accountable, justice will be delivered. That's what I said.

Listen to that, I said that, but they don't show that. They don't show it. They take — they'll take one thing, like, seriously, he was late was the best thing. He was late.

So I said, to anyone who acted criminally in this weekend's racists violence. OK, then I go, we must love each other, show affection for each other, and unite together in condemnation of hatred, bigotry and violence. We must rediscover the bonds of love and loyalty that bring us together as Americans, right?

Then I said, racism is evil. Do they report that I said that racism is evil?"

Denials

(No other president* in history does denials as ... frequently. His hero must be Bart Simpson - "I didn't do it! Nobody saw me do it! There's no way they can prove anything!")

About Saudi King Salman:

"He firmly denies that," Trump told reporters before heading to Florida and Georgia to inspect damage from Hurricane Michael. "The King firmly denied any knowledge of it."
It sounded to me like maybe these could have been rogue killers, who knows. We are going to try to get to the bottom of it very soon. But his was a flat denial."

About Putin:

"President Putin was extremely strong and powerful in his denial today,"

About Roy Moore:

"Roy Moore denies it. That's all I can say. He says it didn't happen, and you know, you have to listen to him also."

"He denies it. And, by the way, he totally denies it."

About Rob Porter:
"As you probably know, he says he's innocent, and I think you have to remember that. He said very strongly yesterday that he's innocent."

About Michael Cohen making payment to Stormy Daniels:
"You'll have to ask Michael Cohen. Michael is my attorney. You'll have to ask Michael."

Less than 20 minutes after seeming to acknowledge that Russia helped him win election:
"No, Russia did not help me get elected . . . You know who got me elected? *I* got me elected. Russia didn't help me at all."

About Jessica Leeds, who accused Trump of groping her on a plane:

"Believe me, she would not be my first choice, that I can tell you," he said to laughter and applause in Greensboro, North Carolina. "That would not be my first choice."

After saying this at a rally: "If you see somebody getting ready to throw a tomato, knock the crap out of them, would you? Seriously. Just knock the hell — I promise you, I will pay for the legal fees. I promise. I promise.", he said:

"I don't condone violence. I never said I was going to pay for fees."

About E. Jean Carroll accusing him of rape:

"I'll say it with great respect: Number one, she's not my type. Number two, it never happened. It never happened, OK? "Totally lying. I don't know anything about her. I know nothing about this woman. I know nothing about her. She is — it's just a terrible thing that people can make statements like that."

About Kim Jong-un denying having tortured Otto Warmbier:

"He felt badly about it. He felt very badly. He tells me that he didn't know about it and I will take him at his word."

Also, a pair of tweets about the Otto Warmbier situation: (spelling here is accurate)
"No money was paid to North Korea for Otto Warmbier, not two Million Dollars, not anything else. This is not the Obama Administration that paid 1.8 Billion Dollars for four hostages, or gave five terroist hostages plus, who soon went back to battle, for traitor Sgt. Bergdahl!"

And:

"President Donald J. Trump is the greatest hostage negotiator that I know of in the history of the United States. 20 hostages, many in impossible circumstances, have been released in last two years. No money was paid." Cheif Hostage Negotiator, USA!

About the chants at one of his rallies when people chanted "Send her back":

"I was not happy with it. I disagree with it. I didn't say that - they did."

"No collusion. No collusion."

Last Words...

(Only for this volume. I know that there will be a continuing supply of such "smart", "great", and brilliant words over the coming years...until there are no more.

8-21-19
"In my opinion, you vote for a Democrat, you're being very disloyal to Jewish people and you're being very disloyal to Israel. And only weak people would say anything other than that. I think that if you vote for a Democrat you're very, very disloyal to Israel and to the Jewish people."

10-27-19
About the death of al-Baghdadi:
"He died like a dog. He died like a coward." Then about the K-9 soldier Conan:
"Our K-9, as they call- I call it a dog, a beautiful dog, a talented dog- was injured and brought back. We had nobody even hurt- and that's why the dog is so great."

"We wiped out the caliphate, 100%. I did in record time."

11-5-19
Rally in Kentucky

"And we will also protect you with pre-existing physicians. How about that? Pre-existing physicians. The first time I've ever said that. Just thought of that! It's true because under their plans, you don't get your own doctor. You know what you get? Whatever the hell you get. That's what you get. Oh great doc, fix me up doc. You mean you want to work on my heart? Who are you, doc? I don't think so.

"Thanks to our tireless efforts to secure our Southern border, illegal crossings have dropped 60% since May. The wall is being built. It's going up rapidly. It's got a big impact. And I want to thank Mexico. We have 27,000 Mexican soldiers on our border policing our border because the Democrats will not do anything to end loopholes. It would take us 15 minutes and we could end the loopholes. Think of the word loopholes. They don't want to end the loophole. If you want to keep violent criminal aliens out of your communities, you have only one choice tomorrow, and that's to vote for Matt Bevin.

"You got to get your friends, you got to vote. Because if you lose, it sends a really bad message. It just sends a bad, and they will build it up. Here's the story. If you win, they're going to make it like ho hum. And if you lose, they're going to say, Trump suffered the greatest defeat in the history of the world. This was the greatest.
You can't let that happen to me!"

July 23, 2019
To students
"Then, I have an Article II, where I have to the right to do whatever I want as president*. But I don't even talk about that."

"Somebody had to do it. I am the chosen one. Somebody had to do it."

(I do not understand what his problem is with dogs…)
"She lied like a dog."

"I see her barking like a dog."

"A lot of people choke. They choke like dogs. They can't breathe.. uhhhh"

"I'm watching Marco sweating like a dog on my right"

"He was run out of office like a dog."

"He died like a dog."

"My call was perfect."

"Read the transcript!"

Closing Words.
Mine.

One might think that with all the available material that I have had to choose from, that it would be so simple, or easy to assemble all of this. You would be wrong. Actually, it is the exact opposite.

Because this president** provides so much quotable material, the hard part is selecting the quotes that would make the most sense. But...not in a literal sense.

But the foundational question was always 'what is he really saying'? What I realized was that much of the time, even he didn't know. At least consciously.

The thought that I would like to leave with the reader is, do the same thing. Ask yourself that same question!

There is too much at stake to leave voting to someone else because we're busy, or to cast a protest vote just because we might be angry. We can still function as a democracy with a few dysfunctional representatives in Congress, but the effect of a dysfunctional president* can last years or even decades.

The office of President of the United States of America is the most powerful position in the world. We cannot continue to have discord and division based on which side we are on, and choose a president that way. We need to have differences and discussion- let the best ideas win. We cannot succumb to the dumbing down of the presidency.

The President needs to be someone who respects our history, all of our people not just a "base", our Constitution, and all of our laws not just the convenient ones, and won't manipulate them.

Enjoy this and thank you.

The term president, with asterisk is borrowed and full credit to Charles Pierce, writer for Esquire magazine.

ABOUT THE AUTHOR

This is the second volume of quotes made by Donald Trump that the author, Leroy Mould, has assembled. He is just one of the millions of Americans that have observed the developments that have taken place in the United States of America over the last thirty or forty years with concern and alarm. He was raised in a politically active conservative home as a child and young man. His father was very involved in politics and his profession in real estate in California in the sixties and seventies. But the author, coming of age in that turbulent time, became disillusioned with how our political atmosphere has become so bitterly divided. He hopes a little levity might help to bridge that enormous gap between left and right.

Made in the USA
Middletown, DE
17 January 2020